The Uses of Ecstasy: Rit Wicca

It is based somewhat on a case study of the Congregationalist Wiccan Association of British Columbia (CWA-BC), a church with five public Temples (in Vancouver, Campbell River, Vernon, and Nanaimo) incorporated in 2004 as the provincial affiliate of the CWA of Canada, founded in 1991, which also has an Alberta provincial affiliate. CWA-BC sees itself as an Outer Court (public) version of Wicca and most Temples are more-or-less British Traditional. I am a founder and clergy member of the CWA-BC but am not speaking for the church in this book and any conclusions which I draw are mine alone, neither approved nor disapproved of by the CWA-BC.

I would like to thank my dear friend Kate Rogers, whose editing labours greatly improved the title section of this book.

And I am forever grateful to the Gods for giving me the opportunity to serve Them.

An Explanation and Understanding of Wiccan Ritual: Approaching a Deviant Religious Discourse in the Modern West © Samuel Wagar 2004 (*Illumine* Vol. 4 Number 1, 2005)

The Wiccan "Great Rite" - *Hieros Gamos* **in the Modern West** © Samuel Wagar 2008 (*Journal of Religion and Popular Culture* XXI (Summer 2009).

The Uses of Ecstasy: Ritual and Practical Mysticism in Wicca © by Samuel Wagar 2010

The Uses of Ecstasy: Ritual and Practical Mysticism in Wicca

By Samuel Wagar MA, 3rd

Obscure Pagan Press
2012 c.e.

Introduction

There is a tendency ingrained deep in our culture at large and in academia to separate the unconscious and creative and the logical and rational. Depending on which side of the cultural divide you fall, either the pragmatic and earth (plebian) or the spontaneous and creative (airy) will be decried or exalted. It is, of course, a false distinction, really amounting to a difference in emphasis rather than differences in type.

In the study of religion it has influenced the branching of subdisciplines. One key branching, which I intend to bring to a synthesis in my discussion, is that between liturgy/ritual and mystical/prophetic experience and understanding. In Wiccan religious understanding, clergy are both mystics and Priestesses, ritual performers and composers, religious innovators and interpreters. The important distinction here is between Initiates and the uninitiated.

I will be examining the forms of ritual and the use of ecstatic possession trance and other stages of trance in Wiccan ritual in general but with a particular focus on clergy training and training toward Initiation. Wicca began as an occultist Mystery tradition practiced in small closed groups by Initiates, and this form of the religion still seems to me to be the core, with the Outer Court movements of neo-Pagans that have grown up around the core through public circles and Wicca 101 classes and through the festivals/religious retreats and social sharing of techniques and ideas from a range of different New Age, neo-shamanic, folkloric and reconstructed paths as secondary developments and influences.

By accepting mystical experiences as normal and fairly common, although prized and useful, and using them as inspiration and fuel for ritual development and further exploration in both the ritual and mystical, rather than thinking of them as grand revelations from the Goddess granted to only a privileged few, the Wiccan approach democratizes the mystical, to the benefit of all in the religious movement. The techniques of ecstasy are seen as not marks of gurudom but as techniques and experiences potentially available to everyone who does the work to master them and is open to receiving the experience.

This is not a manual or handbook of the "become a mystic in ten easy steps" variety. It takes considerable work, dedication and time to become a mystic, able to enter and leave those trance states easily and to bring what you capture of the fire back to the benefit of your community. As well, each Wiccan Tradition has a different mixture of practical skills, knowledge and ritual experience involved in its training. But the broad outlines and the way that the Wiccan approach meshes all three of ritual, magick and ecstatic experience can reasonably be discussed here.

At one point, about ten years ago, when Ronald Hutton's *The Triumph of the Moon; a History of Modern Pagan Witchcraft* was published I was struck by a strange phenomenon. As an academically inclined person (I have an MA in History) and a Wiccan High Priest (3rd degree), it had only seemed natural and completely unremarkable that an accomplished historian might write a history of the origins of the Wiccan religion and the developments in British culture which contributed to its ideas. Hutton's book is an excellent history, rather conventional in its form, marshalling an impressive amount of evidence (all properly footnoted and contextualized) and I have thoroughly enjoyed it in both my initial reading and subsequent ones.

But there was a huge fuss in the Pagan community and the rise of a whole bloc of what must be characterized as "fundamentalist Wiccans" who denied the history to hold onto the occultist myth of the Ancient Hidden Tradition. The same phenomenon has emerged in the feminist spirituality community around the Myth of the Ancient Matriarchy and specifically the speculative work of Marija Gimbutas and also the obsolete Cretan Snake Goddess[1] and Catal Huyuk Matriarchy theories. I was astonished. What we decry in other religions is blossoming in our own, without the same amount of critical commentary. This archaic occultist historical speculation about the "antique wisdom occluded or suppressed by centuries of European civilization"[2] has been standard fare in the occult community for hundreds of years, frequently sliding directly into fascist conspiracy theories.

By examining our true history and choosing to base ourselves on evidence, by discarding outdated theories, we do not thereby discard the poetry, the mythology, the symbolism. The Mysteries are not secrets – secrets are relatively unimportant matters of fact, which any person can find out, whereas the Mysteries are processes through which meaning unfolds, available only to those who have had certain experiences and have done the work to tease out their meanings. By

---

[1] Kenneth Lapatin *Mysteries of the Snake Goddess ; Art, Desire, and the Forging of History* (Boston: Houghton Mifflin, 2002) deals with the early twentieth century invention of Minoan civilization and several of the signature artifacts, particularly the "Snake Goddess" figurine. Joseph Alexander MacGillivray *Minotaur; Sir Arthur Evans and the Archaeology of the Minoan Myth* (NY: Farrar, Straus and Giroux, 2000) deals with the principal inventor of the myth of the Minoans.

[2] Leon Surette *The Birth of Modernism; Ezra Pound, T.S.Eliot, W.B.Yeats and the Occult* (Kingston: McGill-Queen's University Press, 1993), 38. Surette's literary and historical analysis of the connections between occultism and the birth of modernist arts and literature in the fin de siècle is fascinating.

honestly and critically examining our rituals, practices and history, by bringing the critical skills of scholarship to bear we ground ourselves more firmly and we bring more skills to our understanding. Even if a few secrets get told, the Mystery remains, untouched.

Or perhaps I'm just not very good at keeping secrets, those big deep profound spiritual secrets that separate the Initiated Wise from mere mortals, those secrets that I have heard exist somewhere. And I like to do things out in the open, I've never liked hiding away in the broomcloset or pretending to be something I'm not – I'm lousy at role playing games, especially when those games are supposed to extend into mundane life. So there are some parts of the Wiccan and Pagan community where I will never fit in. I'll never fit with those who confuse secrets with Mysteries. Or who find their magickal name and persona a way to insulate themselves in daily life – outside the circle, I am very rarely ever "Lord Whosit" and I think that's how it should be. And those who spend more time burnishing their lineage and being 'special' than doing practical work to help people out.

Yes, I keep secret whatever's told me in Circle, and the names of people who coven with me are held sacred. But I will say I meet in coven and I will say how many members my coven has or my Tradition (as best I know), and I will say what Gods I worship, and I will do public services for people of my faith. I will work to marry, to visit them in hospital and I will work toward full civil liberties for Wiccans. I see those things as a part of my calling as a Priest. My church, luckily, is not about secrets, but about service. We are not about a secret elite (or those with fantasies of being a secret elite, anyhow), but about open and transparent commitment to the Gods and our communities.

In the wake of Hutton, through the opening in the universe of ideas that his book made, numerous other scholars have begun to work in the nascent discipline of Pagan Studies. As a minor worker in that vineyard, I will be applying both the skills and understanding of scholarship I gained in the academy and understandings from my mystical and Priestly training in this book. I am not deliberately setting out to ruffle feathers, but it will please me if some gatekeepers who have deliberately kept their underlings in ignorance are discomfitted by this book, if those who have used talk of the Mysteries to Lord and Lady it over the uninitiated get knocked down a peg or two. "The rituals shall be half known and half concealed: the Law is for All"[3]. On a positive note, however, my principal intention is to look at our training and our mixture of ritual, theology and mystical direct experience and illuminate it, see what kinks or strengths there are in this approach so that we can do it better.

Let me begin by saying that my theology is very much a pragmatic matter. I am interested in what works rather than wasting my time searching for an absolute truth that may not exist, that is non-testable when I might believe that I am next to it, and that has no immediate practical utility. It's not that I don't believe in love and truth and beauty, among other things, but that they are revealed in practice, as we experience them and work to realize them, and not in grand and sterile abstractions. In this I cheerfully follow the Marx of "Theses on Feuerbach"[4] – I am nothing if not eclectic in my influences.

Lore and Tradition

---

[3] Aliester Crowley *The Book of the Law* (New York; Samuel Weiser, 1979), 22.

[4] Karl Marx "Theses on Feuerbach" in *The Marx Engels Reader* (2nd edition) edited by Robert C. Tucker (New York: Norton, 1978), 144.

The Wicca-based religious movement has an accumulated body of lore, including stories, history, rituals, songs, dances, myths and theology.[5] It really has several bodies of lore, which are inspired by the same things but which have grown separately, for each of the main approaches to our common religion. Groups of believers and practitioners accumulate these common songs and stories which have value and meaning and are useful to them, but which are less useful to people that do not share their fundamental beliefs and assumptions. These bodies of lore are self-reinforcing and internally consistent - that is, parts of it refer to other parts of it, although it is not monolithic and closed - authors quote each other, rituals refer to particular works, particular myths and stories are referred to much more often than others and so on. And so gradually different bodies of lore become more and more distinct – Reclaiming folk sing some songs and tell some stories that British Traditions don't or that Ceremonial Magicians don't.

In the Wicca-identified Paganisms, there are already several such bodies of lore, which overlap but which are distinct. Those inside these specific communities can use these bodies of lore more effectively to accomplish spiritual connection and goals for themselves than those outside. People read the same books and practice in the same way - what is usually happening is adaptation and variation of themes within established bodies of lore rather than the creation of brand new ways of doing things. This, I believe, is a very good thing, since brand new things are superficial matters of style until a number of people have been able to work with the new body of lore and deepen it.

---

[5] Sabina Magliocco *Witching Culture; folklore and neo-Paganism in America* (Pennsylvania: University of Pennsylvania Press, 2004). Magliocco's discussion of folk process in neo-Paganism is fascinating and very valuable for me in understanding the interaction between Inner Court and Outer Court.

In Wicca we have a strong feeling that one should create one's own traditions. I would have to say that this "freedom" to create ones own is substantially an illusion and is one of the ideological assumptions of this stream of things. There are unquestioned assumptions of the "what everybody knows" type included in what we do (and I will pick away here and there at a few of them in this book). The discussion of Whitehouse, later on, will look into some of this process of the creation and inculcation of complex theological assumptions into ritual as ways of creating an "everybody knows" about ideas that are, in fact, rather counter-intuitive and complex. [6]

Bricolage[7], as frequently practiced in Wicca, is an effective and conscious technique for ritualization, in particular in a secularized culture such as ours. We make our own culture strange by no longer privileging its ritual forms and religious understandings but placing it into a context in which other cultures may be seen to have effectively solved problems that we are still grappling with. But in pulling these disparate elements together we sometimes lose track of our foundation in the Mysteries. We need to say positively who we are, and not just that we aren't Christians (or whatever - we are not Christian, but we are also not Buddhist or Rastafarian, which means very little, since Buddhism, Christianity, and Rastafarianism have little in

---

[6] Hanne Blank *Straight: The Surprisingly Short History of Heterosexuality* (Boston: Beacon Press, 2012), 25-27. Blank has a very good discussion of the folk process of the creation of "common knowledge" / doxa, and its capacity to reinforce social norms by creating a discourse, in her case about sexuality, that is partial and inadequate.

[7] A term introduced by Claude Levis-Strauss in *The Savage Mind* trans John Weightman, trans Doreen Weightman (Chicago: University of Chicago Press, 1968) to mean improvisation using the materials at hand and adapting them to the task or story, so that myth is both rational and improvisatory.

common). We also need to avoid the unitarian error of subsuming or glossing over real differences.

Individuals demand the authority to define themselves in all areas of life but we also desire community, family and meaning as members of social groups, and desire the pleasure of communion with others that are like us. This can go to the extreme of tribalism, sometimes, but each of us will acknowledge some need for common belief and experience. Which means, defining ourselves WITH others rather than continuing to pretend or try to have total control over what constitutes a Wiccan for ourselves alone. This doesn't mean imposing our definitions on anyone else, but it does mean thinking about what are reasonable boundaries to draw around our body of lore – what are the things that are certainly Wiccan ideas and practices, likely to be included, not so likely, and not included, so that we can go deeper and not just sprawl out wider.

And it's rather like Motherhood – those definitions that absolutely everyone can agree on fall very short of what anyone would base their personal or group practice on: the texts, the rituals and other lore, the techniques of magick, trance and the rest of it, who the authorities that they cite in support of their version of Wiccan practice and so on. For example - probably someone who, like me, cites Crowley, Gardner, Farrars, Hutton, has a different religious practice and understanding than someone who cites Buckland, Cunningham and Silver Raven Wolf. Both are Wicca-based Pagans. But without some way of accumulating and passing on a body of lore, nothing consistent can continue. So we will need to think about and act on this need to gather together and 'invest' cultural capital[8].

---

[8] Pierre Bourdieu *Outline of a Theory of Practice* trans. Richard Nice (1972, Cambridge: Cambridge University Press, 1977). Bourdieu is the principle theoretician of cultural capital.

I think of our religion as properly a 'community of communities' rather than a collection of individuals. Those who feel that Wicca is a purely individualistic path which should be centred on solitary practice are right to be suspicious of me, because that's not what I'm about. Let me be clear that I am answerable to the members of my church and coven and to the Gods, not to the larger Wicca-based Pagan milieu. I disagree with many of them about organization, and also, it seems to me, around this question of a body of lore.

All religions are not simply variations on One True Religion. Buddhist Nirvana is not Christian Heaven, Karma is not The Will of God, salvation through grace is not enlightenment, submission to the guru is not listening for the still small voice of God within and on and on. And the Wiccan ways cannot just borrow undigested bits and pieces of other people's religions and end up with anything that fits together and works for us on our terms. We need our religion to produce answers and practices that help individuals, families, and communities cope with difficult times and create meaning in their lives so they can be more effective in accomplishing their goals. Religion is a project of groups of people, not just a matter of individual inspiration (inspiration is vitally important as energy, but trance and Drawing Down give us energy to create meaning with, not meaning by themselves).

The traditional lore and customary practices are not the creation or property of any individual, even if individuals originally wrote songs or rituals, or were filled and inspired by a Goddess or God. It is when a group of people takes up these things and uses them that they become meaningful. The amount of religious creativity in the Wiccan movement is truly admirable, but the amount of sifting and making patterns out of it, settling on customary ways of understanding and interpreting it, is slower to develop. In true folk culture cultural creation happens in a context and people are able to critically evaluate production in terms of previous work and community needs. That is what I want to have people think about – what works well in our Temples, covens and personal practice and how can we deepen it?

I don't want us to surrender autonomy, but just to accept the need to co-operate and collaborate and for joint ownership of what we come up with together. But this is not an argument with other Wicca-identified Pagans. I am interested, in my writing, to describe a facet of the present and work toward the future- how shall we see our religion and how shall we see our future? Are we to see ourselves needing to incorporate aspects of another religion and its ideas to fill in the gaping holes in our understanding or do we just need to more clearly understand tools and practices already part of our own? We will need to draw upon the experiences and insights of other religions faced with the same problems, but we should not adopt their solutions without translating them into our terms.

Some Wiccans believe, along with Dion Fortune, that "All Goddesses are one Goddess, All Gods are One God, and the Two are One in Love." In this vein we often hear people speak of "The Goddess" and "The God" as standing in for the female principle and the male principle, for Shri and Vishnu, creativity and its realization, energy and matter. But these generic forces cannot have enough distinct personality to develop a relationship with – just as my friends have names and I have loved and lived with individual women (not "All Women"), so my relationships to the divine are personal. I believe that the Goddesses and Gods share the quality of divine power, that purity of focus and intention, the unchanging quality of eternity, and perhaps also gender, with each other, but they are otherwise distinct Beings who relate with me, or not, as They individually desire.

Because the Gods are not well served by generic, dispassionate recognition or by rote performance of rituals and obligations, although such recognition is part of the duty of a Pagan religious person, as an expression of general piety which pleases the Gods,[9] specific Gods impose specific demands. A passionate life, one that involves the Gods, is so much more satisfying for human beings and passionate devotion to the Paths of our Matrons and Patrons will develop us as human beings and as Pagans. Ginette Paris' and James Hillman's books are powerful descriptions of living in the service of, as embodiments of, our Gods, although from a Jungian, not Wiccan, perspective.[10]

Where do we want to go? How are the Goddess and Horned God, and all of the Old Gods, talking to us? When we gather together in our communities and worship the Great Mother, what do we feel and what does She say? Great Artemis, Noble Apollo, boisterous Pan, gentle Qwan Yin, Tiamat of the mysteries of the waters, All Father Odin, come in answer to our call – your children have need of you

In the Names of Aradia and Cernunnos, Blessed Be

---

[9] For an interesting discussion of this issue, Plato *Euthyphro Dialogue* from 380 BCE deals extensively with the question of piety in a polytheistic culture (ancient Greece). It is discussed later on.
[10] Ginette Paris *Pagan Meditations: The Worlds of Aphrodite, Artemis and Hestia* trans. Gwendolyn Moore (Dallas TX: Spring Publications, 1986) and *Pagan Grace: Dionysos, Hermes and Goddess Memory in Daily Life* trans Joanna Mott (Woodstock CT: Spring Publications, 1990), James Hillman *A Terrible Love of War* (New York: Penguin Press, 2004).

An Explanation and Understanding of Wiccan Ritual: Approaching a Deviant Religious Discourse in the Modern West

Wicca is a modern religion, based on occultist ideas, founded in the mid-1940s in the United Kingdom but now widespread in the English-speaking world. This book deals principally with the core of the Wiccan religion – the small group based religion which defines Wicca as an initiatory Mystery religion practiced by clergy - rather than the broader "Outer Court" neo-Pagan movement that has grown up around it, influenced by it but also somewhat independently of it.

The origin myth of Wicca as being substantially a survival of pre-Christian ideas of the indigenous northern European or Celtic religions has been thoroughly discredited by modern historical scholarship, although a minority of fundamentalist Wiccans still hold to the myth instead of the history.[11]

All religions begin at some time and place as new religions, or deviant religious movements, and thus act as vehicles for social critique and, if they are

---

[11] Ronald Hutton, *The Triumph of the Moon: a History of Modern Pagan Witchcraft*, (Oxford: Oxford University Press, 1999). Hutton is the best single history of the cultural developments in the United Kingdom over the past couple of centuries leading into the founding of the Wiccan religion.

successful, social change. It follows that the study of deviant religious movements, particularly new ones, involves issues central to all religions.[12] In this chapter's discussion of Wicca as a deviant new religious movement the deviant religion is viewed as a healthy creative project, inspired by the spirit.

Deviant religions can act as heterotopian sanctuaries for the exploration of new discourses[13]. They can accumulate spiritual capital for their members through fruitfully expressing an aspect of the tensions of the larger society, capital that is dependent on both internal forces of the religions and the larger society's response to the discourses developed inside and spreading out from these deviant groups. This spiritual capital can be mobilized for other purposes, as for instance where a number of feminist women involved in Wicca have mobilized capital accumulated through the religion into political activism. [14]

Wicca is a deviant religion in the modern West. In contrast to the dominant religious tradition, Christianity, it is polytheistic or duotheistic, feminist

---

[12] Aidan Kelly *Crafting theArt of Magic Book 1: A History of Modern Witchcraft 1939-1964* (St. Paul MN: Llewellyn Publications, 1991) , 3

[13] Michel Foucault "Of Other Spaces" trans. Jay Miskowiec *Diacritics* 16.1 (Spring, 1986), 22-27
A heterotopia is a "place outside of all places… different from all the sites that they reflect and speak about" and such sites are counter-cultural locations for the expression and exploration of denied facts of social reality, which invert some norms in order to explore them and then feed back into the dominant culture, either as a means of exposing and contesting ordinary reality or as a perfection of the confusion of ordinary relationships.

[14] Bradford Verter "Spiritual Capital: Theorizing Religion with Bourdieu Against Bourdieu" *Sociological Theory* 21.2 June 2003, 150-174. Verter defines 'spiritual capital' as "religious knowledge, competencies, and preferences as positional goods within a competitive symbolic economy" whose valuation is the "object of continuous struggle and is subject to considerable temporal and subcultural variation." 150

with matriarchal tendencies (with Priestesses taking
slight precedence over Priests, the Goddess over Her
Consort), panentheistic[15], ecstatic, hedonistic and nature-
centred. It is a small religious movement that is growing
very rapidly – between 1981 and 1991 the number of
Pagans counted in the Canadian census grew from 2295
to 5530 and by 2001 to 21,085.[16] Because of its
intersection with the feminist political movement and the
reinterpretation of female spirituality, Wicca can
legitimately be described as a counter-hegemonic
movement based on gender issues. The original rituals of
the religion will be shown to express this contra-
hegemonic sensibility.

Polytheology and Ethics

A religion is not just a set of beliefs or symbols,
not simply a category of facts, but a way of being in the
world, a way of knowing, and a way of making
knowledge. It engages in various types of exploration,
experiment and explication around this knowledge
making (perhaps more accurately, *meaning-making*)
process. In addition, religion rests upon a tension
between that which is (Be-ing) and that which is
potential (Becoming) and much religious practice
assumes the primacy of the future. The great religious
and ethical question, "How should I live to be a good
and ethical person?" has a different outcome for people
like Wiccans, following a polytheistic religion without a
single Holy Book, than what we've been taught. This is,

---

[15] John Bowker ed, *The Oxford Dictionary of World Religions*
(Oxford: Oxford University Press, 1997) defines panetheism on page
730 as the view that "the world exists in God ... but God is not
exhausted by the world; the divine is both transcendent and
immanent."
[16] Statistics Canada, Ottawa, 1981, 1991, 2001 Census of Canada.
The majority of Pagans are Wiccan , so these numbers are likely to
reflect the proportionate growth in the Wiccan population.

however, a question that religious people of whatever religion have to grapple with, and so I'm going to take a few minutes here to explore it.

For Wiccans, I suggest going from that question to asking "Who am I?" and then following that up with "Who are the Goddesses and Gods that are mainly concerned with the type of person that I fundamentally am?" We don't need or want to be anything except who we are, and we don't want to be all like the same 'perfect' person, but we want to be the best and strongest, most ethical, most interesting version of who we are.

Our Gods are not role models that we wish to emulate in every detail. They are powerful and beautiful and obsessively centred in their areas of excellence. They cannot point us toward a happy and balanced life, not as individuals, because They are anything but balanced. They cannot show us an ethical, just and moral way of living because They are neither ethical, nor just, nor moral, nor living beings. In the same way as it is absurd to speak of an ethical or moral mountain or the ethics of electricity or gravity, it is meaningless to speak thus of most Gods.

By saying that one is a child of a particular Goddess one takes on Her attributes and affirms Her as central to one's understanding of oneself. One commits to personal development in tune with this Goddess' Way and can expect Her help in developing an ethical and personal style that fits with Her Way. But one must also explicitly recognize the final decision rests with the human side of us. What we need to develop, as we develop Wiccan ethics and ways of being together is a model of human excellence that we can aspire to. We need a model that is not a single person, because each person differs in needs, capacities, and tastes and one size does not fit all. We need a model, moreover, that fits well with the individualistic streak of Paganism and that respects our need to be moral agents and to make individual ethical choices.

This key goal of discipleship is important, assisting individuals to become like the Gods – establishing the conversation of our Holy Guardian Angel and finding the Goddesses and Gods that want to work with us individually and also collectively, while remaining true to our humanity.[17] We must live our values, acting in all parts of our lives as the embodiment of the good and the virtues. Modelling by clergy is crucially important and the quality of leadership is directly proportional to the quality of discipleship. If we fail in this key task of assisting people to embody their Gods, then we fail, essentially.

Other Paths, other ethics and other mores are also valid and legitimate Paths. One person's Goddess is not necessarily important in another's life and the values and behaviours that She demands of Her devotees are not necessarily anything that anyone else should be concerned with. In the broader shared sense, the sense of "How I should live my life together with other people," ethics and morality are human agreements, not Universal Truths Handed Down From Olympus, or whatever. "The archetypal tolerance of polytheism – each god, each goddess entails another. They are all enfolded together in the great bed of myth, and their tolerance is essential to their natures."[18]

---

[17] Alan Hirsch *The Forgotten Ways: reactivating the Missional Church* (Grand Rapids MI: Brazos Press, 2006). This challenging, erudite and provocative book has had a great influence on my work. Hirsch is a fundamentalist and evangelical Christian. As well as Hirsch, Aliester Crowley's *Liber Samekh* in *Magick in Theory and Practice* (1929 reprinted New York: Dover 1976) and Ginette Paris' excellent books are inspirational and very helpful.

[18] James Hillman op cit, 205

This problem of how the Gods fit in with ethics and morality was dealt with in 380 B.C.E. by Plato in the *Euthyphro Dialogue* between Socrates and Euthyphro, a classic philosophical text that is still very useful. The following question, among others, is posed: "Is an action wrong because the Gods forbid it or do the Gods forbid it because it is wrong?" Trying to resolve the question can be done in two ways, which lead to different conclusions, both of which are more or less a problem for the monotheist or for those who believe that the Gods are the source of ethics and morality : a) "The Gods forbid an action because it is wrong" – this admits that there is some standard of right and wrong that is independent of the Gods and that wrong actions were already wrong prior to Gods forbidding them; or b) "An action is wrong because the Gods (or a God) forbid it" – the position required to reduce ethics to religion.

In the first case we look to the universe or to human nature, not to the Gods, for the source of good and evil. In the second case we end up with three unacceptable positions: (i) Morality is Contingent. So any action that is actually wrong could have been morally right, including, say, acts of torturing innocent children for fun, if a God approved of it (and there are few actions that one God or another does not approve of). (ii) The Gods' Commands are Arbitrary. If things aren't right or wrong or good or bad independent of the Gods' commanding or forbidding them, then there is no good reasons to choose what to command and what to forbid. (iii) The God's Goodness is Trivial and Therefore Not Praiseworthy. If whatever a particular God prefers is thereby automatically best, then the fact that she/he always prefers the best is a trivial fact, true merely by definition. But then always preferring the best does not make Her/Him praiseworthy.

Socrates also talks with Euthyphro about differences of opinion among the Gods, but, falsely in my opinion, accepts that the Gods ultimately agree with one another. This dodges around the simple polytheistic ethical way out of the problem – because the Gods differ, different ethics result from relationships with different Gods, and our ethical choices ultimately must come from ourselves and not from Them. We adopt ethics that come from our nature and potentials as human animals and our membership in particular societies. The Gods reinforce capacities already possessed by us, and deepen us in tune with our shared natures.

Polytheistic religious frameworks do not provide an absolute list of ethical and moral guidelines beyond some foundation statements. There is no single set of rules and guidelines for all people but a great variety. The great Greek Pagan philosopher Aristotle came up with an ethical system and model 2400 years ago that is still suited to these needs. Aristotle argued that we don't need ethical systems that list rules, does and don'ts, or that try to deal with every conceivable question. People are different and there are simply too many situations to ever have a perfectly exhaustive list of responses, and rigidity and rules based behaviour is not natural, rational nor spontaneous or beautiful.

His idea of virtue ethics gives a great variety of moral ways to live depending on the kind of person that one fundamentally is and the agreements that one makes with one's Gods to help develop oneself. Some absolutes like the preference to avoid harming other people, respect for a range of different Gods and different means of being devoted to them, and honesty about ones actions and choices are important in the Wiccan path as well.

What we need, instead of rules, said Aristotle, is to develop strength of character. A person of good character will naturally choose to do what is right under whatever circumstances they are presented with. They will have a well-developed sense of appropriateness, appropriate to them, not necessarily to anyone else, and will consistently act in tune with the good. The means to develop strength of character, said Aristotle, is to understand that there are virtues that can be cultivated, effectively like developing a series of good moral and ethical habits. By developing the habit of always doing the right thing, we will respond to any situation by doing what is right in that situation.

Aristotle is fundamentally healthy in his ethics: the goal of ethics is completely practical and concerned with good human functioning here in the world, with living the good life, which he considers to be the happy life, the soul in accordance with reason. Aristotle came up with lists of virtues like courage, generosity, public-mindedness, friendship and so on, but he did not, importantly, say how exactly these would be expressed for a given individual, or claim that these lists are complete.

Although he excluded some actions that are never good in any amount what he also did that was significant was he said that virtues are the actions and the passions occupying the middle path between two extremes, each of which is a vice – one being too much expression of the action and the other too little. For example, although generosity is a virtue, giving away everything that you own is a vice, as is giving far less than you can afford. Each of us, however, must find what is virtuous to do and to find the balanced middle ground of correct action that expresses the virtues in tune with our nature and circumstance. Ideally we shall also enjoy doing what is right - we are virtuous not because of rules but because the good life gives us more pleasure.

So we have here a positive model of right action to aim toward, one that is in tune with the basic ethical precepts of Wicca and that can include devotion to particular deities. Although the servant of Aphrodite will behave differently than a devotee of Quan Yin or of Odin or Mars, all can be ethical people and pursue the good life. People need not aim toward a rigid adherence to a list of rules, but rather may seek to become people with strong understanding of themselves and good personal ethical codes who can be trusted to behave appropriately under any circumstances. [19]

Aristotle's ethics do not seek to limit our pleasures or to deny the body or the spirit. Instead we are required to choose and to take responsibility for our choices. It is based on the understanding that what you do, you are. By choosing to lie, you are a person who lies and it becomes easier for you to remain dishonest than to become honest. By not standing up for what you believe to be true you become a coward. But the vices of cowardice or greed or untrustworthiness are flaws of personal character, not flaws in the universe or "the Goddess made me do it." Vices can be overcome by changing your character and by becoming the kind of person that you want to be.

Aristotle doesn't give us any kind of an easy out from our ethical responsibilities, nor a simple set of rules. What he gives us, writing as he was from within a polytheistic Pagan framework, is a dynamic process and a system of mutually reinforcing virtues and vices. Like the Gods need to be understood in and through their relationships to each other rather than as all-powerful singular figures, no one virtue is complete, and no one person is complete without community. By adding a

---

[19] Brendan Myers *The Other Side of Virtue* (Winchester UK: O Books, 2008). A contemporary Druid philosopher's book on virtue ethics which examines not just Aristotle but also the heroic virtues og the Norse religion.

sense of the virtues to the ethics of "an ye harm none" we know not only what we should not do but what we should do and how we should go about doing it. Even more importantly, we learn who we should be, whatever we are doing.

Some History and Religious Studies

By positioning religious knowing as just one, non-privileged, type of knowing and by redefining religion as plural, the secularization of the West in the 19th century and subsequently both opened up religious knowing and denied its exclusive truth claims. By becoming able to comparatively study contradictory truth claims, the absolute truth of a given religion's claims is denied. Wicca, a magical religion, is centred on the creation of experiences and states of mind, on truth games[20] rather than on truth claims, aside from the claim about the general value of these experiences or states. In this it resembles a mystical path or *bhakti* yoga practice of worship through devotion rather than the legalistic Abrahamic religions' emphasis on structures. This is less directly in conflict with the secular.

The social particulars of religious expression are necessary aspects of its existence, but these details do not exhaust religion. Social constructionist theories may be better at explaining why people will choose mainstream non-deviant religions and how they are

---

[20] Tanya Luhrmann *Persuasions of the Witch's Craft: Ritual Magic in Contemporary England* Cambridge MA: Harvard University Press 1989. Luhrmann's chapter 22 on "Serious Play: the fantasy of truth" pp. 324-326 is a very effective exploration of the element of play and 'truth games' in Wiccan contemporary practice. Alex Owen, *The Place of Enchantment: British Occultism and the Culture of the Modern* (Chicago: University of Chicago Press, 2004) deals very effectively with the magical imagination in chapter five "Occult Reality and the Fictionalizing Mind" pp. 148-185.

conditioned and disciplined by these religions, but falter when dealing with religions of converts, non-mainstream faiths like Wicca. The order of society is shaped by the mainstream; the fundamental institutions from the family through the educational system to the governmental structures are all steeped in the religious and moral values of the dominant religious traditions. The conversion experience still exists for mainstream religions and religious meaning is still extracted from their rituals and theological discourses. The person involved in the mainstream religion is able to be as devout as one involved in a deviant religion yet the cost of involvement in a mainstream religion is less than in a deviant one, and the reinforcement of its values is constant and partly external to the individual and the religious institutions. For a deviant religion to continue and to grow, it must be more effective in producing rewards for its members and must mobilize spiritual capital more effectively.

Stark and Bainbridge argued in *The Future of Religion* that religions are a means to produce and distribute non-material goods, spiritual compensators in the form of blessings of character, happiness, community, and assurance of life after death, which are more valuable if the amount of work gone into producing them is greater, as in a deviant religious movement in some degree of tension with society. These compensators are valuable regardless of access to material rewards.[21] Pierre Bourdieu's analysis of cultural capital as a medium of social relations has been developed by Bradford Verter into an alternative economic model for the use and exchange of spiritual goods that is better able to account for the particular

---

[21] Rodney Stark and William Bainbridge *The Future of Religion: Secularization, Revival and Cult Formation* Berkeley: University of California Press, 1985. Compensators are defined on page 6 as "the belief that a reward will be obtained in the distant future or in some other context which cannot be immediately verified."

goods produced and exchanged in deviant religions than the Stark's model, because Bourdieu's ideas include the relations of power and their negotiation within the religious movements.[22]

Dipesh Chakrabarty states that "gods are as real as ideology is – that is to say, they are embedded in practices. More often than not, their presence is collectively invoked by rituals rather than by conscious belief."[23] This quotation points to a key difficulty in historical recovery of religious experience – the need to go beyond the texts to recover the beliefs and experiences imbedded in practice, and to accept the viewpoints of religious people as being valid. Practices and rituals, particularly of popular religion, are less well documented than the elite theological exegeses. When we speak of religions as animated by the Gods and spirits that work through them we honour the perspective of the worshippers.

Those theories that reduce religion to one or the other social factor, which assert the universality of an economic class, race, gender, or ideological factor above the reality of the divine assumed by the practitioner, do violence to the autonomy of the subject and disregard the agency of the religious person. These factors do enter in, and must be included to fit the religious projects in with other social forces. But the religious person is not required to accept the primacy of the secular or to understand her actions through that lens. With a Wiccan panentheistic sensibility, which sees deity through its manifestation in society and in the world, the social utility of religion is an aspect of its divinity and the

---

[22] Verter, "Spiritual Capital ..."

[23] Dipesh Chakrabarty *Provincializing Europe: Postcolonial Thought and Historical Difference* Princeton: Princeton University Press 2000, 78. I recommend Chakrabarty's chapters 3 ("Translating Life-Worlds") pages 72-96 and 4 ("Minority Histories, Subaltern Pasts") 97-113 highly as serious attempts to balance belief and history and to bring suppressed histories based on belief into the rational.

Goddess as an advocate for the equality of women and men is not reduced from the divine but expressed as the divine active in the world through people. The influence of Wicca in the feminist movement is due in part to this religious understanding, just as was the occultist spiritual influence into first wave feminism.[24]

Issues specific to deviant religions point to the boundaries of some theories of religion. The use of religion as a social control mechanism for enforcing discipline and control over the subaltern classes is challenged by the conversion of people away from the normal religion of their society. The boundaries of the society itself are challenged by these conversions, to the extent that the society is defined as having a particular religious values centre[25]. Wicca, a small religion rapidly

---

[24] A complete bibliography of Wicca's intersection with feminism is beyond the scope of this book, or the capacity of the author. Significant texts include: Robin Morgan, *Going Too Far: The Personal Chronicle of a Feminist* (New York: Vintage/Random House, 1978); Margot Adler, *Drawing Down the Moon: Witches, Druids, Goddess-Worshippers and other Pagans in America Today* (Boston: Beacon Press, 1979); Starhawk *The Spiral Dance: A Rebirth of the Ancient Religion of the Great Goddess* (San Francisco: Harper and Rowe, 1979); and Zsuzsanna Budapest *The Holy Book of Women's Mysteries* (Oakland: Susan B. Anthony Coven , 1979). Scholarly work of note includes Tanya Luhrmann *Persuasions ...* op cit; more extensively in Susan Greenwood, *Magic, Witchcraft and the Otherworld: An Anthropology* (Oxford: Berg, 2000); Helen A . Berger, Evan A Leach, and Leigh S. Schaffer *Voices from the Pagan Census: A National Survey of Witches and Neo-Pagans in the United States* (Columbia SC: University of South Carolina Press, 2003) and Janet Dahr, *Wild Women Witches of Greater Vancouver: Gyn/Ecology*, an unpublished M.A. thesis in the Department of Women Studies, Simon Fraser University, 1995. Insight into the role of the occult in first wave feminism can be found in Joy Dixon, *Divine Feminine: Theosophy and Feminism in England*, (Baltimore: John Hopkins University Press, 2001), 3. "A feminist spirituality was a crucial component of much feminist politics..." and Ann Braude, *Radical Spirits: Spiritualism and Women's Rights in Nineteenth-Century America* (Boston: Beacon Press, 1989).
[25] Gauri Viswanathan, *Outside the Fold: Conversion, Modernity and Belief* Princeton: Princeton University Press, 1998. Viswanathan

growing through conversion, is producing spiritual capital and challenging this social cohesion.

The different religious goods valued in the deviant religious movement challenge a simple and universalist idea of religion. These are ideas less valued in the dominant tradition and indicate different audiences and needs. Establishing religious authority, the authority of particular texts and practices and of particular individuals and theological positions, is more difficult in a deviant religion, particularly a new religious movement, because of the need to negotiate which ideas one values and why and how they fit together, or don't.

As well as the issues involved in the study of all religions, and of deviant religions in general, there are issues involved in the explanation and understanding of Wiccan ritual particular to the situation of the Wiccan religion and to its assumptions and approaches. These include the centrality of the ritual in Wicca, the expectation of religious creativity and fluidity, and the small group norm, coupled with ecstatic practices.

If mythology emerges to explain ritual and theology arises in order to explain mythology then, where possible, study of religion must go back to ritual.[26]

---

deals with several conversion narratives in this way. Particularly telling are her chapters four, "Silencing Heresy," 118-152, which deals with the hybrid experience of Pandita Rambai and the ways that her experience revealed the polyphony inside the Western and Christian identities, and seven, "Conversion to Equality," 211-239, dealing with the mass conversion of Indian dalits (untouchables) to Buddhism led by Ambedkar.

[26] This formulation is developed from Robertson Smith, *Lectures on the Religion of the Semites,* First Series, *The Fundamental Institutions.* Burnett Lectures. 2nd Edition, London page 19 as cited in Hans G. Kippenberg, *Discovering Religious History in the Modern Age,* translated Barbara Harshaw (Princeton: Princeton University Press, 2002), 75. "So far as myths consist of explanations of ritual their value is altogether secondary, and it may be affirmed with confidence that in almost every case the myth was derived from the

The intellect makes sense from an experience or artwork, but it does not make meaning. As religion is primarily in the business of making meaning, not so much of making knowledge or pragmatic common sense, the structuring done on the level of ritual performance, aesthetic and emotional, is the primary experience and the codification of it is secondary.

The historian seeks to understand change over time. The Wiccan religious perspective is that the divine expression is always conditioned and contingent, a particular expression through specific individuals at a particular time and place. It is thus compatible with conventional history. As "every man and every woman is a Star"[27] (an expression of the divine) rituals that reinforce and express this belief like *Drawing Down the Moon and Sun* and the *Great Rite*, are central. The divine remains eternal and immortal through the fact of its dialectical engagement with the temporal, an insight expressed through the *Charge of the Goddess*, one of the nearly universal pieces of Wiccan liturgical poetry, as "I am the soul of nature, who gives life to the universe."[28]

The standard form of Wiccan ritual began with the composition of the first rituals by Gerald Gardner and associates in 1947. These rituals circulated in manuscript form and were modified by successive associates of Gardner, notably Doreen Valiente, prior to being described and published in part in Gardner's *Witchcraft Today* (1954) and *The Meaning of Witchcraft* (1959). The history of the successive versions of these rituals has been established by Aidan Kelly in his

ritual , and not the ritual from the myth; for the ritual was fixed and the myth was variable, the ritual was obligatory and faith in the myth was at the discretion of the worshipper." This is consistent with Tanya Luhrmann, *Persuasions*. Op cit, chapter 22, 324-326 in particular.

[27] Aliester Crowley *Magick* xiv
[28] Janet and Stewart Farrar *Eight Sabbats for Witches* (London; Robert Hale, 1981), 43.

Crafting the Art of Magic Book 1; A History of Modern Witchcraft, 1939-1964.The streams of British occultist and counter-cultural thought that influenced Gardner and associates have been examined in detail by Ronald Hutton in *The Triumph of the Moon: a History of Modern Pagan Witchcraft.*[29] This book will rely substantially on the chronology established by these two scholars.

The Wiccan origin myth, which is still literally adhered to by a minority of practitioners, but which remains symbolically important to many others, has Wicca as a direct lineal descendant of pre-Christian European fertility religions, both Celtic and British or from the aboriginal Stone Age cultures immediately after the last Ice Age. During the period that Gardner and his associates were starting the religion, Gardner's *Witchcraft Today* was published (1954) and he there put forward several variations of this origin myth, speaking of "the witch who is a descendant of a line of priests and priestesses of an old and probably Stone Age religion."[30] He also indirectly credits many of his sources in the book: Aliester Crowley, Rudyard Kipling, the Hermetic Order of the Golden Dawn[31], Hargrave Jennings, Francis Barrett, and Margaret Murray, who provided the preface to the book.[32] He also mentions by indirection the origin of the spiral dance ritual and meeting dance: "it may

---

[29] Aidan Kelly *Crafting* op cit; Ronald Hutton *Triumph* ... op cit.
[30] Gerald B. Gardner, *Witchcraft Today*, London; Robert Hale 1954, reprint New York: Magickal Childe, 1982.
[31] The Hermetic Order of the Golden Dawn was a ceremonial magical order that grew out of the esoteric Masonry of the *Societas Roscicruciana in Anglia* in 1888. It was by far the most significant English occult order, and drew prominent intellectuals and talented ritualists to it. It collapsed in internal wrangling in 1900. Ellic Howe, *The Magicians of the Golden Dawn: A Documentary History of a Magical Order 1887-1923* (London: Routledge and Kegan Paul, 1972) is an xcellent history of the Order.
[32] Gardner, *Witchcraft Today*, 47-8

simply be an old children's game which the witches have taken over or vice versa."[33]

The following briefly situates Gerald Gardner through the years leading up to 1954, when the basic rituals of the Wiccan religion were being written: He was a heterosexual, married, middle-aged man who had lived overseas in the south Asian part of the British Empire (Sri Lanka, North Borneo and Malaysia) for much of his life as a plantation manager and then an inspector in the Malayan customs service. He retired to England in 1936, at the age of 52, a knowledgeable occultist and 'joiner,' who belonged to a range of associations involved with folklore and the occult. After becoming involved in several aspects of the British occult scene, he embarked upon the development of Wicca in 1947. He was in many ways well prepared to provide an expression of various cultural forces that had been accumulating in British culture over the previous two hundred years and thereby to create a new religion. [34]

Gardner was a high ranked member of the Ordo Templi Orientis, the Ceremonial Magical Order headed by Aliester Crowley. He was involved in the Rosicrucian Theatre in Christchurch in southern England, which was an offshoot of the Theosophical Co-Masonry movement, and many of his associates in his first covens were drawn from this group. He was a nudist, member of a naturist club near St. Albans, Hertfordshire, and built a 'witch's cottage' on land adjacent to it for his coven meetings. He was a member of the Folk-Lore Society and author of a well-received book on Malay ritual knives entitled *Keris and Other Malay Weapons* (1936).[35] The range of occult and folkloric influences that he was able to bring to bear on the creation of the Wiccan

---

[33] Gardner, *Witchcraft Today*, 141
[34] Hutton, 239
[35] Gerald Gardner *Keris and Other Malay Weapons*, B. Lumsden Milne ed. (Singapore: Progressive Publishing Company, 1936).

religion is dealt with fully in Hutton and need not be elaborated upon here.[36]

However, new religions are founded every day. The Wiccan religion has been modestly successful in its growth, despite a strong bias against proselytizing and a training period before new members are able to participate in rituals, and it has been highly influential in raising issues that are now also concerns of other religions. Wicca has brought forward consciousness of the Goddesses and divine feminine, the sacredness of pleasure and of the body, the sacredness of nature and ecological consciousness, and promoted the usefulness of ritual and the creation of rites of passage. Aside from the intrinsic interest of the new and creative religious expression, attention must be paid to details of the content of the rituals and the religion.

Summary of Standard Gardnerian Ritual Script

A Priestess, usually assisted by a Priest whom she chooses, leads the rituals. The Priestess, as the embodiment of the Goddess, is explicitly primary, although the male principle is included in ritual as well. Rituals are performed in the nude and include a small group of celebrants of both sexes, known as a coven. There are explicitly sexual aspects to the foundation ritual and the "Great Rite", which is not performed at each coven meeting, is a *hieros gamos* (sacred marriage rite). These aspects are transgressive of gender norms today and were more so in the immediate post-World War Two period from which the first authenticated Wiccan ritual manuscripts date. [37] The central ritual of Wicca is *Drawing Down the Moon* and it will be dealt

---

[36] Hutton, 205-240
[37] Hutton, 238

with in detail throughout this book. It is a ritual of possession trance, which aims to bring the Goddess (or, usually, A goddess) to come into and occupy the body of the Priestess for the duration of the coven meeting. A God version, *Drawing Down the Sun,* is performed less often.

A careful read through the earliest version of the standard Wiccan ritual from 1949[38], established by Aidan Kelly, reveals its textual influences and origins. The ritual has been adapted since then, but the pattern established in the original coven is still the norm.

The Wiccan ritual has the features of a formal opening and closing of the boundaries of the ritual space, which is typically only open to initiated members of a small worship group (in Wicca, a coven), the suspension of ordinary time and the aspect of critical reflection outside of time, space and culture. The transgressive element is marked first by the requirement for ritual nudity of all participants, save for jewellery and marks of rank in the religion. It establishes the ritual space as a heterotopia, conforming very well to Foucault's discussion of the term as a space set aside for the intensification of cultural differences, conflicts or social options. Heterotopian sanctuaries allow the focused development and working out of social facts and may or may not later be reintegrated into society as a whole as catalysts for social change. [39] Because heterotopias are set aside they do not necessarily affect the larger society.

Numerous details of the ritual are Masonic or derive from classic works of the Western Ceremonial Magic traditions, although they are creatively adapted to suit the circumstances of the Wiccan religion. The set-up

---

[38] *Ye Bok of Ye Art Magical* manuscript in Wiccan Church of Canada collection, Toronto. Kelly gives a detailed breakdown and analysis of this material from pages 47-75.
[39] Michel Foucault , "Of Other Spaces" 22-27.

of the ritual circle is adapted slightly from the medieval grimoire *The Key of Solomon the King*[40], a popular text among occultists in England. A circle is marked out, nine feet (2.7 metres) in diameter with two outer circles around it separated from the first by six inches (15 cm) and one foot (30 cm). Names of deities are written in the two rings surrounding the inner circle. The perimeters of the circles are traced by the ritual leader with her *athame* (knife used in ritual). There is then a blessing of water and of salt, which are mixed together and with which the circle is asperged. The wording of the water and salt purifications used in Wiccan ritual is very similar to that found in *The Key*[41] although asperging with salt water is also a Roman Catholic and Anglican tradition. Candles are lit at each of the cardinal directions with a blessing.

The *Lesser Banishing Ritual of the Pentagram*, a ritual derived from the Order of the Golden Dawn, is then performed. The ritual leader makes the gesture of the Cabbalistic Cross by touching, in turn, her forehead, chest, right shoulder and left shoulder and then clasping her hands in front of her while intoning "Ateh (thou art), Malkuth (the Kingdom), Ve-Geburah (and the power), ve-Gedulah (and the Glory), le-Olam (for ever), Amen." She then turns to each of the cardinal directions in turn, beginning with the east and going clockwise, draws a pentagram (a five pointed star with one point upward) in the air with her athame and calls out the deity name associated with that direction: Yod He Vau He, Adonai, Eheieh, and Agla. Then, standing with arms outstretching in the form of a cross in the centre of the circle she says; "Before me Raphael, behind me Gabriel, at my right hand Michael, at my left hand Auriel. Before me flames the Pentagram, behind me shines the six-rayed star." She again makes the Cabbalistic Cross as

---

[40] *The Key of Solomon the King,* S. Liddell MacGregor Mathers, trans and editor (London: George Redway, 1888; reprint New York: Samuel Weiser, 1974), 17-8.
[41] ibid 90-91.

before.[42] This part of the ritual is explicitly Christian ceremonial magic, with Cabbalistic trappings – calling upon Christian names of God and angels, the ritual leader crossing herself, and the Cabbalistic translation of part of *The Lord's Prayer*. [43]

Finally the ritual leader will walk three times around the circle, clockwise, turn and address each direction in turn and call for the spirits of those directions to come and participate in the ritual. This originally Christian Ceremonial Magical ritual has been simplified, and partly de-Christianized, in order for non-Christian folk magic to be worked.[44] The substantial use of the Cabbala, derived originally from Jewish mysticism, has been a mark of the British occult community since its introduction in the 1740s, although the magical Cabbala is very different from the mystical one.[45] The five elements of Earth, Air, Fire, Water and Spirit and the five directions which are generally associated with them North, East, South, West, Centre are considerably more than the literal things and directions.

What they are is symbolic containers for a number of important ritual and human ideas and processes, and a set of associations and correspondences that differs with each person, although covens will have an agreed language to address them. Because the elements are such broad categories it's possible to both tailor one's understanding of them to fit well with what

---

[42] Israel Regardie, *The Golden Dawn*, 1941, reprint 6th edition St. Paul MN: Llewellyn Publications, 1989, 53

[43] Matthew 6.13

[44] Aidan Kelly, 51

[45] Joscelyn Godwin, *The Theosophical Enlightenment* (Albany: State University of New York Press, 1994). Godwin's excellent history of the Anglo-American occult traces the development of Christian occult Cabbalism in far more detail than possible here, beginning on page 94.

individuals need and believe and at the same time be able to communicate something of that to others.

Beginning with the directions – these four cardinal directions, by being recognized and called after the circle is cast, make the circle into a symbolic "World in Miniature" – here is the North, the East, West, South, and when the Centre is called, here is the entire universe. The circle becomes the centre of the universe, even more it becomes the central axle or pole which the rest of the universe revolves around, which holds everything else together. By calling the directions Wiccans transform "a place that is not a place" into "ALL places" and identify their actions here with the actions of the Gods at the beginning of time and the end of time.

This universal place that is created is a place without character, "without form and void" – by calling the elements it is given shape and meaning and filled up with the potential for creation. By recognizing the elements outside of the ritual space they speak to the qualities in the universe that they most value, to the creative potentials imbedded in everything, the fluid capacity of water, the inspiration of air, the rapid change and development of fire, the ability to make dreams real of earth and the deeper meaning of the spirit.

Wiccans can and must layer associations over top of one another – speak of the elements not like a chemist would talk about calcium, but as poetry. So air that is clear and moves, sustains our life, blows with the rising sun and thus signifies both the beginning of day and the start of life, including within it all beginnings – a much more evocative and emotionally satisfying image and layered response. Identifying these elements explicitly with both the events of their lives and their physical, carnal, selves, making them direct participants in the creation and maintenance of the universe.

Following the casting of the ritual circle,
Drawing Down the Moon is performed. *Drawing Down*
is a ritual of ecstatic possession trance. Its purpose is to
assist the Priestess to embody the spirit of the Goddess
of the Wiccan religion, one of Whose most prominent
symbols is the Moon. It is the ritual of incarnation in
which the divine becomes human and present in and
through our bodies. She opens herself up, surrenders her
body in trust, to become inhabited by an awake and
aware Goddess. For a short time, generally only a few
minutes, her body is the body of a Goddess. While she is
more or less aware and in control, there is another
Presence there during that time.

How does this work? What is the theology and
the technique? First: Our bodies are sacred and holy.
They are individually specific examples of the divine
potential to create, to move and to express itself through
matter. The world is not fallen away from grace and
neither our bodies nor our spirits are contaminated or
evil. Second: our bodies have particular abilities and
senses which give the divine pleasure. Our pleasures and
our experiences interest and engage the Gods. They like
to experience reality through our bodies. Third: The
Gods, or at least particular Goddesses and Gods, are
interested in being involved with people and with our
lives, and some are interested in each of us, and in our
specific lives. Some Goddesses and Gods have an
emotional or erotic interest in us, and some are just
friendly. We are worthy, worthy because the Gods want
to come and be with us, worthy because we want to
serve the Gods, and worthy because we will become
better people through Drawing Down.

As an experience, Drawing Down ranges from a
mild sense of "presence" – heightened awareness of
oneself and the rest of the Circle – through deeper levels
of sureness, to dictated messages, visions, and on to full-
scale Possession Trance in which the Priestess' ordinary

consciousness is suspended and the Goddess uses her body as a vehicle. There will be a thorough discussion of these stages later on. With an experienced partner guiding one into the ritual, surrendering oneself to it, it is completely safe. An experienced person will know how to bring the Priestess back to ordinary reality if she is uncomfortable.

The symbol of the pentagram is drawn on her body by the Priest, through touching her with a phallic-headed wand while reciting an invocation, the Five Fold Blessing. Although the specific points touched are not specified in the document, current practice is at neck, left hip, right breast, left breast, right hip and neck again[46]. His invocation incorporates a quotation from Crowley's *Gnostic Mass* ; "By seed and root and stem and bud and leaf and flower and fruit we do invoke Thee."[47] He then kisses her feet, knees, lower belly, breasts, and lips while reciting a blessing; "Blessed are your feet, which have brought you in these ways, …your knees, that shall kneel at Her sacred altars, … your womb, without which we would not be, … your breasts, formed in beauty and in strength, … lips, which shall speak the sacred Names."[48]

He begins by sanctifying the body of the Priestess, by blessing the individual person as uniquely sacred and uniquely qualified to act as the vessel in to which the divine will pour itself. These invocatory gestures and statements explicitly establish the sacredness of the female body, and specifically the body of the individual Priestess receiving the blessings and being asked to embody the Goddess. Although the person is blessed as an individual and individually

---

[46] Janet Farrar and Stewart Farrar *The Witches' Way: Principles, Rituals and Beliefs of Modern Witchcraft* London: Robert Hale 1984, 69.
[47] Crowley, *Magick …*, 350.
[48] Kelly, 52.

sacred, they also are identified, in the Five Fold Blessing, with the universal – this body is all bodies that have been blessed in this way, this is the Body that expresses the human face of divinity. The blessing of the genitals and breasts, the ritual nudity, as well as the use of the phallic wand in the blessing, emphasize the overt sexuality and carnality of this embodiment, as do the ritual kisses. The body is sacred here, *because* it is a body, not *despite* its carnality. The identification of the woman's body with nature does not involve the association of nature with a lesser spirituality as conventionally assigned, but is an identification of the type of divine power being called – the immanent divinity of the forces of nature, the force of fertility, sexuality and the body. This blessing is specifically erotic. It is not sexual, not directed toward genital sex for sure, but it awakens the tactile sense and the physical awareness, heightening this awareness in order to ground the experience.

The Priestess wakes the body up fully, extends her sense of touch and expands the aura, in this safe place in Circle. Then she takes this vessel that has been blessed and opened and gradually fills it with the sense of the divine. The series of blessings will have relaxed the Priestess and made her open and receptive. Inside all of us there is a sure feeling of connection to the infinite, to the underlying causes and supports of the universe. By relaxing and letting down our guard we bring this awareness and connection closer to the surface, we open the door and give permission to fill ourselves, or be filled, by the divine. We must both invite the Goddess in (and it is a personal decision how open we can be, how safe we feel, not anything that can be forced even in the smallest amount), and relax away from the fear of being harmed or overwhelmed. It is not ever completely easy or free from fear to surrender control to the circle, your working partner and the Gods, but it is necessary. We can have the Goddess open our eyes, hear through our ears, move with our body and speak with our voice. And we are changed by this, made better people. That is why Wiccans do it.

The Priestess, now seen as embodying the Goddess, recites the *Charge of the Goddess*, a central theological statement of Wicca. It begins with a syncretic list of Goddesses from various times and places, all identified as aspects of the Great Mother: Artemis, Astarte, Aphrodite, Cerridwen, Bride, and others. Then a lengthy section adapted from *Aradia: Gospel of the Witches* by Geoffrey Leland in which the Goddess asks Wiccans to assemble once a month, preferably on Full Moon[49], to "be free from slavery, and as a sign that ye be really free, ye shall be naked in your rites, both men and women"[50], to dance, sing, feast, make music and love[51] in Her praise. Then follows a quotation from *Book of the Law* which includes the phrase "nor do I demand aught in sacrifice"[52] and other material adapted from *Magick in Theory and Practice* by Aliester Crowley, and particularly from the *Gnostic Mass* (Liber XV).[53] There is some original material in the Charge, including the significant phrase "all acts of love and pleasure are my rituals"[54], but slightly more than half of it is reworked from Aliester Crowley.

The other Wiccan material that was written at this time includes the originals for the three Initiation rituals. Although the current practice is that the three rituals are separated by periods of time, typically a minimum of a year of practice and training, the original rituals were set up to be performed one after another on the same occasion.

---

[49] Charles G. Leland, *Aradia or The Gospel of the Witches*, 1890; reprint Custer WA: Phoenix Books, 1990, 6, cited in Kelly, 53.
[50] Leland 6-7, cited in Kelly 53.
[51] Leland, 14, cited in Kelly, 53.
[52] Aliester Crowley, *The Book of the Law*, 26 cited in Kelly, 53.
[53] Crowley *Magick,* 345-61.
[54] Kelly, 53.

For the First Degree the Postulant is brought into the ritual circle blindfolded, hands bound together and the ends of the rope brought around the neck in the Masonic manner with the cable-tow being used to lead him around the circle to be presented to the spirits of the four directions. He is blessed, put through a short ordeal (bound and ritually scourged) and then administered an oath before being untied, having his blindfold removed and being presented with the ritual tools of Wicca. For the Second Degree he is blindfolded, blessed, put through a short ordeal as before, administered an oath, and then told to use the ritual tools, prompted where necessary. He then is required to scourge the Priestess as instructed, as a demonstration of his new power and responsibility. For the Third Degree the Priestess is scourged, then scourges the Postulant, as a ritual of purification. Then the ritual of the *Great Rite*, which is a ritual of sexual intercourse as worship, *hieros gamos*, is performed.

There are numerous borrowings from Masonic ritual in the First Degree, including the use of the cable-tow and hoodwink (blindfold) and many phrases in the obligation oath are directly copied from its *Entered Apprentice* ritual. The presentation of the ritual tools is also a detail taken from Masonic sources.[55] A number of details are also patterned on the Order of the Golden Dawn's *Neophyte Ritual*, although enormously shortened and with the language and ritual equipment substantially simplified.[56]

---

[55] Kelly, 63-4.
[56] Regardie *Golden Dawn*, 117-133.

Sexuality in Ritual Symbolism

We may briefly contrast the sentiments in this central theological statement (*The Charge of the Goddess*) with those expressed in Christian tradition. This is particularly telling when we consider that the period immediately after the Second World War, the period of the birth of Wicca, saw a dramatic revitalization of British Christianity, of domestic ideology and the rebirth of the "Angel in the House.[57]" The Wiccan "acts of love and pleasure" sharply contrasted with the sexually unassertive woman whose "desire shall be for your husband, and he will rule over you."[58] Wiccan ritual nudity contrasted with the general Christian attitude, but echoes the theme of Genesis 3, that unashamed nudity symbolized innocence. The leadership by women in Wicca contrasted with the Christian norm, after the deutero-Pauline epistles, that "I do not allow a woman to teach or exercise authority over a man, but to remain quiet."[59]

Kelly argues that Gardner emphasized scourging and a highly scripted form of sexual ritual in order to satisfy his personal sexual needs and that otherwise there is "no reason to include scourging in the ritual."[60] Hutton was able to examine Gardner's books, including his modest collection of pornography, and found that "none of the pictorial or literary items in the books is concerned with binding or flagellation,"[61] which leads him to conclude that Gardner was not introducing this

---

[57] A popular Victorian trope drawn from Coventry Patmore's poem of the same name celebrating love and marriage, 1854-6.
[58] Genesis 3.16
[59] 1 Timothy 2.12
[60] Kelly, 65.
[61] Hutton, *Triumph,* 235.

element for that reason. Although Frederic Lamond, who was a member of Gardner's first coven in 1957 talks of him as "an unashamed and somewhat innocent sensualist" who was obsessed with binding and scourging as the only method by which he could reach an altered state[62]. The extensive ritual use of scourging as a form of purification in ritual is not found in any of the Masonic sources, but the use of *hieros gamos* in initiation and in ritual is found in the Ordo Templi Orientis, the ceremonial magical order to which both Gardner and one of his literary sources, Aliester Crowley, belonged. The O.T.O. had ceased to function in Britain by the late 1940s although Crowley's books were popular among occultists.

This sacralization of sexuality and of sexual intercourse is highly transgressive in the context of late 1940s England, and remains so today. Although there is a great deal of variation among modern Wiccans, the basic form of ritual established in 1949 continues. The use of the scourge and of *hieros gamos* has been greatly reduced, with the majority of Wiccans accepting these things as legitimate aspects of Wiccan practice but not personally engaging in them. However, ritual nudity, the use of kisses on the body during *Drawing Down*, the ritual of *Drawing Down the Moon*, the general form of the Initiation rituals and many other ritual ideas from Gardner's first covens are prominent features in contemporary coven practices, de-emphasized or absent in public rituals. The Wiccan religion has changed from a religion of small groups, all of whom were Initiated Priesthood, to a variety of traditions all drawing elements from the same roots but not practicing in the same way. This polyvocality was established as a norm by Gardner and continues as a prominent feature of Wicca.

---

[62] Frederic Lamond *Fifty Years of Wicca* (Sutton Mallet UK: Green Magic, 2004), 10-11, 98.

Ritual nudity told Wiccans that they are bodies and is a valuable challenge to ego boundaries.[63] The erotic is made clearly a sacred force through many details of the ritual. *Drawing Down* is explicitly about immanence and trance and the possibility of prophecy. Bringing to the ritual the assumptions about the body and sexuality from the broader society led to a challenging and redefinition of those things. The awkwardness of the initial involvement with this ritual style, the discomfort with nudity, the weak and ineffective experience of trance the first few times its practiced, gave way through habituation and the construction of a stronger and more defined magical personality[64], to a more effective and graceful performance. The small group norm makes this learning less difficult because of immediate feedback and lesser performance anxiety. As Luhrmann points out, "people often argue for a belief as a means to legitimize, and even to understand ... the practice in which they have become involved."[65] The practice of the ritual produced resultant experiences that were then made sense of and made into beliefs.

Some provocative research undertaken in Canada by Shelley Rabinovitch found that virtually all of the active participants in the Wiccan religion had been emotionally, physically or sexually abused as children or adults, in most cases in more than one way.[66] This study

---

[63] Lamond, 96

[64] Luhrmann *Persuasions...* Her chapter 21 on "Interpretive drift" 307-323 is an excellent description of the process of application of magical ideas which leads to a comfort with them, an ease in the use of the symbolism and ideas of the Wiccan and magical worldview.

[65] Luhrmann, 310.

[66] Shelley Tsivia Rabinovitch *An Ye Harm None, Do What Ye Will: Neo-Pagans and Witches in Canada* unpublished MA Thesis, Department of Religion, Carleton University, Ottawa 1992.Rabinovitch found that 39 of the 40 women and 20 of the 27 men whom she interviewed in taped interviews reported experiences of abuse. 98-114.

indicates that the transgressive aspects of Wiccan practice acted as means to bring forward the feelings of participants in a psychodrama and heal them from their abuse. It is possible that these data can be projected backward, carefully, to the origins of Wicca as well. The high rates of abusive families hidden behind the ideological façade of perfect domesticity have only recently been brought forward. The Patriarchal monotheisms have been inadequate in religiously dealing with or even in acknowledging the extent of familial disfunctionality. In the discursive climate of the origin of Wicca, with the reified family and Freud both influential, this factor may well have been important.

The non-material compensators produced through Wiccan ritual, to return to Stark and Bainbridge, include the re-valuing of the body, the re-emphasis of personal sexual power and efficacy, and the identification of the individual with the divine. The specific form of social capital that has been produced through the Wiccan religion has been the capital which feminist women, in particular, are able to draw upon – the emphasis on the special sacredness of women's experience, of the female body and of the Goddess and rituals and art celebrating these things. Although only a minority of feminists are Wiccan, there is less reinterpretation of the beliefs and symbolism necessary for Wiccan social capital to be mobilized by them than for those feminists in some other religious traditions. With the second wave of feminism beginning in the late 1960s, this capital became valuable in the larger society. In addition, the original heterosexual exclusivity of Wiccan symbolism has shifted somewhat with the rise of gay and lesbian movements to an emphasis on generally sex-positive spirituality, mobilizing another type of compensator and spiritual capital.

The Initiation by Gardner of Doreen Valiente at Midsummer 1953 was a significant turning point in the development of Wicca. Valiente was an intelligent and gifted writer who became Gardner's High Priestess and substantially revised the rituals, elaborating on fragments, and reworking the awkward wording of the earliest versions, plus removing some of the more obvious Crowleyana[67]. Even at the earliest date another aspect of Wicca, which distinguishes it to the present, emerged – Gardner's "insist [ence] that all Wiccan initiates should not merely copy the existing rituals and statements of belief but alter and add to them according to their own tastes and abilities."[68] This insistence on polyphony, coupled with Gardner's disavowal of his personal authorship of the foundation rituals, and his theoretically subordinate position working under his High Priestesses, produced a religion with spokespeople but no prophets. The norm of small group working, coupled with the splits and splinters beginning in 1957 when Valiente and her faction split to form a coven of their own, which continued to operate until her death in 1999[69], further increased the amount of variations on a theme in the liturgy of the Wiccan religion.

This liturgical variety means that unearthing the earliest drafts of the Wiccan rituals is not like the recovery of sacred scriptures, but instead the examination of first drafts of an ongoing process of discovery of the divine involvement in the Wiccan religion. The rituals and stories are all works in progress and express a view of the Goddess and Her Consort centred on continuous revelation and adaptation rather than finality. And by including "leaping laughter" in the *Charge of the Goddess*, as a desirable aspect of devotion, a playful and experimental quality was included from the start. [70]

---

[67] Hutton, 247.
[68] Hutton, 248.
[69] This coven was studied by Luhrmann as part of her PhD research, published as *Persuasions...* op cit
[70] Kelly, 53.

Wicca developed in the modern context, as a religion of well-educated urban Britons and North Americans. Recent survey results indicate that Wiccans are substantially more educated than the general American population, with 64.5% possessing a BA or better while 51% of the American population has a high school education or less.[71] Its practitioners have an ironic and modern or post-modern approach to ritual and belief, drawing on the modern magical traditions of the Hermetic Order of the Golden Dawn and Ordo Templi Orientis. The depth of challenge to the version of scientistic rationality that was developing with the advent of modernity represented by the magical thinking of these Orders continues in the rational mystical experimentation of Wiccan ritual. Alex Owen explores the issue of magical subjectivity in her *The Place of Enchantment* and Joy Dixon in *Divine Feminine* issues of the intersection of the occult with feminism.[72] The influence of both on this author has been profound.

In a polytheology the "God card" does not trump anything. When I say that my Patron, Legba, demands certain things of me, this imposes no requirement on you to do or say anything, since the rules of Legba apply only to His people (and He rewards only His people). In order to persuade you to behave in a certain way, I have to genuinely persuade you of the worth of a particular ethical position and I have to be open to be persuaded myself, since I don't necessarily have a truth for anyone but myself.

We must be in dialogue around morality, rather than giving a set of detailed rules and requiring them. It is not absolutely true, for example, that there is one good

---

[71] Helen A. Berger, Evan A. Leach and Leigh S. Shaffer *Voices ...* op cit, 31-2, particularly table 6.
[72] Alex Owen, *Enchantment*: op cit; Joy Dixon, *Divine Feminine...* op cit.

way to be sexual (or even twenty ways – all that we can all agree on is freely consenting adults) or that there is one diet that our Gods require of us (some Gods are vegetarian, some are hunters, some are herders and shepherds, many don't care, some want animal and human sacrifice) or one attitude toward the use of violence and warfare.

Ethical standards are useful and our common human nature as hierarchic pack-hunting social mammals tells us which areas are important – long lasting pair-bonds and families, order and organized groups with leadership and ownership of resources. But these ethics are not binding on the Gods, and they reflect what we came from but not what we aspire to become, not our joint project with the Gods. If right and wrong differed completely for each individual, building community and organized religion would be very difficult and perhaps pointless (if religion is in the ethics business, which Socrates and I would argue that it isn't necessarily). But things do not differ that dramatically, the Golden Rule does apply, and our relationships with the Gods do not over-ride our ethical autonomy and self-determination – the Gods may be wrong, or lying.

Dialogue and absence of dogma are essential qualities of polytheism. We must co-operate as individuals and as communities to seek the truth, because our Gods are biased as individuals and no one of them has the whole truth. At the same time there is no endpoint to the dialogue, no final conclusions, but rather an ongoing exploration of moral and ethical questions. So, living as a good and ethical person as a polytheist means living in community and in dialogue with others, respecting and learning from their experiences with their Gods.

These ethical questions and our relationships with our Gods are not just individual matters, either, but apply to our Temple work and rituals, to coven work and to how we are as religious people in the larger world.

The Wiccan Great Rite: Hieros Gamos in the Modern West

Although Wicca is a new religion, it draws upon older materials for ritual and theology. Most of these go back no further than the late Victorian United Kingdom but it has, particularly the "Outer Court," since incorporated popular religious and New Age ideas like astrology, folk magic techniques, and a range of alternative healing arts as well as strong influences from feminism and popular culture – in particular science fiction fandom and the Society for Creative Anachronism. The neo-Pagan movement around the Wiccan core emphasizes individualism and nature-centredness even more strongly, and often uses the same symbols and celebrate on the same occasions. There are some substantial differences – a greater influence from the New Age movement in neo-Paganism, for example, and a greater emphasis on beliefs over experiences.

At the centre of Wicca, however, is a truly ancient idea – the *hieros gamos* / sacred marriage. The *hieros gamos* ritual, called by Wiccans *The Great Rite*, is a ritual of sexual magic involving intercourse between the Goddess of fertility, ruler or embodiment of the land, as embodied by Her Priestess, and Her Consort, represented in the king or Priest, said to have been practiced from ancient times into the classical Greek period. The ritual is most often performed symbolically, 'in token', in Wicca-influenced groups and 'in actual' only in private coven workings.

This chapter will begin by outlining the theology and history of the Great Rite then outline Wiccan ritual forms and the specific ritual of the Rite and move onto excerpts from primary documents of Priestesses and Priests reporting on their experiences of the Rite, before concluding.

Through sexual intercourse with the Goddess the king's right to rule is made legitimate in the classical Greek literature. The kidnap and marriage of Helen by Paris was not just an affront to Menelaus as a husband, but undercut his legitimacy as a ruler and precipitated the Trojan War of Homer's *The Iliad*. The attempts of Penelope's suitors in *The Odyssey* to woo her were also connected to Ulysses' rulership of Ithaca.[73] According to Mircea Eliade's *Myth of the Eternal Return*, on the day-to-day level marriage rituals frequently still recapitulate hierogamy, especially the union of heaven and earth[74] and "the cosmic myth serves as the exemplary model not only in the case of marriage but also in the case of any other ceremony whose end is the restoration of integral wholeness ... the cosmogony first of all represents Creation."[75]

The *hieros gamos* continues in the Jewish and Christian mystical traditions of the marriage to God, with the soul as the bride and God as the groom, although without physically being acted out.[76] The route by which the *hieros gamos* came into the English occult

---

[73] A worthy recent treatment using this interpretation is Margaret Atwood *The Penelopiad* (Toronto: Alfred Knopf Canada, 2005).

[74] Mircea Eliade, *The Myth of the Eternal Return*, translated Willard R. Trask, (1954, revised edition Princeton: Princeton University Press 1971), 23.

[75] Ibid, 25.

[76] Jeffrey J. Kripal Roads *of Excess, Palaces of Wisdom; Eroticism and Reflexivity in the Study of Mysticism* (Chicago: University of Chicago Press, 2001) is an excellent study of the erotic mysticism in the Abrahamic traditions.

milieu and ultimately into Wicca began with Sir William
Hamilton and Richard Payne Knight's writing on phallus
worship in the 1770s and Payne's research into the
Orphic Mysteries which gave rise to a significant strain
of esoteric phallicism.[77] Another route was through the
German Ordo Templi Orientis's (OTO) influence from
Indian Tantra and from the American sex magician
Paschal Beverly Randolph, which came to England
through the prominent occultist Aliester Crowley with
his 1912 Initiation into the OTO.[78] The influence of the
OTO into the foundation rituals of the Wiccan religion
was profound.

The sacred marriage affirms the right of the king
to rule and in Wicca confirms and seals the highest level
of religious initiation, 3rd degree, and has the mystical
meaning of a loving union with Godhead. Wiccan
Initiates are taught the skills needed to enter into and
leave, fruitfully, mystical states of consciousness. The
revived interest in mystery traditions and Paganism in
the late Victorian period fed directly into the milieu of
the birth of Wicca. This movement had a more-or-less
neo-Platonist belief in an occluded spiritual realm and a
broad animism in which all is interrelated and part of a
universal or cosmic soul. This, together with a "belief in
the essential unity of matter and spirit and, similarly, a
correspondence between things earthly and spiritual,"[79]
makes "the mystical" mean "occultism". So, reclaiming
the mystical might properly be said to include reclaiming
the occult.

---

[77] Joscelyn Godwin *The Theosophical Enlightenment* op cit, chapter
one, 1-25 deals with theories of phallus worship.
[78] Alex Owen, *Enchantment: ...* op cit, 217. John Patrick Deveney,
Paschal Beverly Randolph, (Albany: State University of New York
Press, 1997).
[79] The term "the mystical" will be used in this book as Alex Owen
used it in reference to the "range of spiritual alternatives to religious
orthodoxy .... a distinctively 'esoteric' turn" that emerged in the
1880s and 1890s. Owen, ibid, 21.

Mystical and Sexual Experience

The mystical experience can be and is, interpreted in many contradictory ways – facets of the experience include both remaining separate but joined, dissolving, both ultimate powerlessness and connection to great power, and being awash in the experience. Some aspects are socially and personally positive and some are corrosive and antinomian. In the Great Rite, the antinomian challenge is to norms of heterosexual monogamy, in particular. The mystical experience dissolves away the boundaries of the individual and permits them to honour themselves as a part of the All. The individual can become aware of themselves as a unique expression of the divine purpose or an integral portion of the universe. By dissolving the ego boundaries an intensity of feeling, a depth of connection, and a kind of meaning is derived. It is terrifying as it begins but it resolves into an immensely reassuring fact as the fear of death and the sense of loneliness dissolves. The existential fact of separateness is momentarily set aside in a fundamental joining.

William James, in *Varieties of Religious Experience*, sets reasonable limits to the authority of the mystical state and provides a thorough discussion of the range of explanations applied post facto to the experience. He also differentiates the mystical experience from the psychotic break or fugue state, both of which it resembles highly, not by the details of the experience but by how the person is changed by it. "Religious mysticism is only one half of mysticism, the other half has no accumulated traditions except those which the textbooks on insanity supply." [80] The mystical

---

[80] William James, *The Varieties of Religious Experience* (1902, republished New York: Barnes and Noble Books, 2004), 368. His full discussion of mysticism is Lectures XVI and XVII, pages 328-371, and he provides valuable points to illuminate the Great Rite in his Lecture XIX, 395-417, and the Conclusions , 418-450.

initiatory experience opens one up in ways different than a mental break but must be tested by the same empirical methods that would be used to evaluate any other experience, and "non-mystics are under no obligation to acknowledge in mystical states a superior authority conferred on them by their intrinsic nature."[81]

There is, after all, no 'pure' experience, only experiences in one context or another, interpreted by the person experiencing them in the light of previous experiences and the expectation of future ones. They are subject both to the past and future and act as inspiration and fuel to further experiment, analysis and creation. By embracing this intertextual quality of mystical experience, its shaping and reference (and self-reference) we can appreciate the mystical not as meaning itself but as provoking meaning-making activity, shaking up and reshaping the configurations of the psyche, although not in a predetermined direction. The mystical is greater than any of the explanations of it.

Abraham Maslow provides a cross-cultural and materialist description of the typical features of the mystical state in *Religions, Values and Peak Experiences*.[82] He affirms the mystical experience as common and deeply meaningful, although inexplicable. He argues that "man has a higher and transcendent nature, and this is part of his essence, i.e. his biological nature as a member of a species which has evolved."[83] The experience does not necessarily point toward a Goddess or God but may be purely biological.

Another perspective on the mystical experience is Dipesh Chakrabarty, cited earlier, whose inclusion of religion and religious experience in history and his post-

---

[81] Ibid, 369.
[82] Abraham H. Maslow, *Religions, Values, and Peak Experiences*, (1964, revised edition New York: Viking Press, 1970).
[83] Ibid, xvi.

colonial challenge to enlightenment materialism is bracing. When we see the Gods as agents in our history, acting alongside and through human beings (even if only insofar as their worshippers attribute agency to them in their actions) a different set of histories emerge, with a greater psychological or sociological insight. Catherine Bell provides a provocative discussion of a number of theories of ritual in *Ritual Theory, Ritual Practice* in the process of developing her own theory of ritual as social production and practice, and Pierre Bourdieu, in *Outline of a Theory of Practice* has a brilliant development of theories of cultural capital and practice (in the Marxist senses, particularly of the Marx of "Theses on Feuerbach"), which both Bell and Bradford Verter draw upon. These scholars are highly useful analytical starting places for this book's discussion. [84]

All of these theoreticians emphasize practice, experience and the pragmatic consequentialist evaluation of experience over the theoretical and ideological. Beliefs are not primary to them because specific beliefs do not predict specific behaviours and vice versa. The fact of belief in general terms is important but practice leads to practical consequences which then spur on belief. This practice-based approach opens up the possibility for a rational exploration of the mystical, an approach to trance and to factors that lead toward the mystical experience and a rational and conscious shaping of the experience and its energy into making meaning useful to the mystic and her or his religious community.

Catherine Bell emphasizes, after Jonathan Z. Smith, that ritual is work, a kind of labour, a social product and a way of making, not something given from the Gods but created by human beings together. Bell has been very important in my understanding of ritual as the

---

[84] Catherine Bell, *Ritual Theory, Ritual Practice,* (New York: Oxford University Press, 1992); Pierre Bourdieu, *Outline* ... op cit ; Bradford Verter, "Spiritual Capital..." op cit.

central activity of religion and a means of making meaning and reinforcing discourse.

Alex Owen, in *The Place of Enchantment,* demonstrates exactly this approach to rational mysticism in the Hermetic Order of the Golden Dawn, an occultist group that was a direct ancestor to the Wiccan religion. She states that "individuals underwent training in the apprehension and negotiation of occult phenomena, and subjective claims were tested and measured against clearly established criteria."[85] These magicians sought a spirituality that was not revealed, but self-consciously created as a joint project through ritual and symbolism utilized as tools for inner exploration.

I am beginning with the study and description of the ritual and experiences reported by people who have undertaken it, rather than a theological exegesis. The intellect makes sense but it does not make meaning. The primary experience of religion is the ritual experience , and the codification of it is secondary. This is particularly true, as Bell claims, because "religious beliefs are relatively unstable and unsystematic for most people."[86] There is a need to go beyond the texts to recover the experiences imbedded in practices, and in order to derive the likely beliefs of practitioners. Practices and rituals, particularly of popular religion, are less well documented than the elite theological exegeses. Therefore, the analysis in this book will be strongly based on ritual scripts and, where possible, first-hand reports of the experience of ritual performance.

The questions that legitimately can be asked of *hieros gamos* include: What can it be in the modern age? Why has it emerged as a central symbol and frequent real practice in a modern religion? What does it say about modernity, anti-modernity and what does the

---

[85] Owen, 148
[86] Bell, 184-5.

practice bring to its participants? What does it say about and how does it inform thinking about sexuality, revelation, the mind-body problem, the sacred and mundane, and the psychology of ritual? How does it relate to conventional morality? What types of power relationships and resistances are expressed through it?

Another question that needs to be asked of the *hieros gamos* in particular concerns the ambiguous relationship between its valuing of sexuality and the female body and the sexual power dynamics in Western culture. When we look at the religions which celebrated the *hieros gamos* in the past, this ritual is linked to strong Goddesses, such as Inanna in Sumer, Persephone and Demeter in Greece, and also to the power of women.[87] The suppression of the ritual coincided with the suppression of women's sexuality and the worsening of an unequal situation for women. The suppression of free sexuality and of women, and the suppression of *hieros gamos*, occurred at roughly the same time in Europe as the Patriarchal era began.

The connection between the Wiccan religion, a feminist-influenced religion, and the practice of sexual ritual then is not unexpected. However, envisioning a free sexuality, and even more one that is connected to spirit rather than separate, requires more than simply ethical archaeology – the experience of sex has been so shaped by the inequalities between women and men, the anti-body attitudes from the Olympian Greeks onward in Western cultures, the Jewish and Christian dethroning of the Goddess[88], the high rates of sexual abuse, and

---

[87] *Hieros gamos* for Inanna is discussed in Diane Wolkstein and Samuel Noah Kramer, *Inanna: Queen of Heaven and Earth*, (New York: Harper and Rowe, 1983), and for Persephone and Demeter in Ann Suter *The Narcissus and the Pomegranate: An Archaeology of the Homeric Hymn to Demeter* (Ann Arbor: University of Michigan Press, 2002).

[88] Susan Niditch *Ancient Israelite Religion*, (Oxford: Oxford University Press, 1997). Niditch documents the archaeology

institutional homophobia and compulsory monogamy
that its reclamation is not simple.

Wicca is a new religion, growing rapidly but not
centred on a charismatic leader, so that its rituals and
practices and its theology are evolving from a
community of believers' experiences rather than a
prophet's individual inspiration. Because Wicca
emphasizes prophetic trance experiences, it could be said
to be a religion of prophets rather than being inspired by
only one. Its links to the feminist spirituality movement,
its role as a critical voice in debates around sexuality and
the equality of women and men, and its creative
syntheses of traditions, all give it an importance greater
than its current numbers. Whether Wicca will serve the
same functions as Theosophy, an ancestor movement to
it, did in the 1890-1920 period, as a creative leavening of
the spiritual and cultural landscape prior to collapse and
decline, remains to be seen.

The Great Rite, *hieros gamos*, is at the centre of
Wiccan ritual and theology. It is an egalitarian erotic
mystical path open to both genders and a variety of
sexual interests, although most often expressed as
heterosexual. Unlike the Patriarchal sacred marriage in
which God is the bridegroom and the soul is the bride,
the Great Rite has a meeting of equal powers through
two equal bodies, with both parties possessed by the
divine, and with a physical acting out rather than purely
an internal or symbolic expression. Unlike those
traditions in which the divine is seen as masculine only,
so that the deepest erotic mystical joining is only
possible for homosexual men and, in those traditions that
allow women mystics, heterosexual women, Wicca
worships a variety of deities with both sexes and all
sexual preferences and genders.[89]

---

demonstrating the existence of the Asherah-Yahweh pairing in
ancient Israel.
[89] Jeffrey J. Kripal, *Roads of Excess, Palaces of Wisdom:* op cit.

The study of religion can centre on a view of religions as ordering systems of law and morality, as communities of worship, as central cultural and political forces legitimating the power of the king or the state, as artistic creations, or as many other things. There are legitimate reasons to argue against the dominance of a mystic focus in the study of religion and to question the motivation of the great emphasis on the mystical in recent history of religions.[90] The mystical paths are seen to be antinomian, attacking structures and laws, overturning morality, and as intensely personal and individualistic. These facets of the mystical experience are directly contrary to the experience of religion as community, even of minority religions as alternative systems of meaning and alternative communities of belief.

However, this critical view of the mystical accepts the individualistic fallacy – if the individual is not created *ex nihilo* but emerges in a social context, individualistic experiences must always be interpreted through a social lens, both in support of and in harmony with the norms or in reaction against them. There is no pure experience, but always an experience which is being reflected upon as it occurs in an intertextual dance with not just other experiences but also other descriptions of them, no pure individual subject but always a social creature, and no experience free of power, resistance, creation and so on. The individual's

---

Kripal brilliantly discusses erotic mysticism and the homoerotic quality as well as the Patriarchal limits placed upon it in the major religious traditions.

[90] As for example in Steven M. Wasserstrom, *Religion After Religion: Gershom Scholem, Mircea Eliade, and Henry Corbin at Eranos*, (Princeton: Princeton University Press, 1999). Wasserstrom deals magnificently with the complex political and occultist factors informing the work of three great names in the history of religions, in particular pointing to occultist and fascist leanings and connections among them and reflected in their work's emphases.

mystical experience, therefore, embodies some social and spiritual capital,[91] and it is an action in society, not just in the psyche of the person experiencing it, through their actions.

In the case of Wicca, mystical actions are explicitly framed as social, and the consequences of them are seen as shaping the whole of the religion and its effects on its adherents and the larger world, even by those Wiccans who do not experience them or who are deemed unqualified to interpret them. The deep experience of the mystical shapes the habitus of the Wiccan practitioner, at least of the religious specialists, and the production of spiritual capital by all participants in Wicca reinforces the forms that are effective in its production.[92]

Although different forms of mysticism exist, the Romantic bent of the Western intellectual has led to the interpretation of the 'real' mysticisms as those individualistic and antinomian aspects.[93] This is unconsciously culturally bound, part of the "things everyone knows" – in some other cultures there is group and community ecstatic and public mystical experience – in Voodoo and the other Afro-diasporic religions of South and Central America for important examples.[94] By

---

[91] Verter, 150-174.

[92] "Habitus" is defined by Bourdieu as "a lasting, generalized and transposable disposition to act in conformity with a (quasi-) systematic view of the world and human existence." Pierre Bourdieu, "Legitimation and Structured Interests in Weber's Sociology of Religion". Translated by Chris Turner, in *Max Weber: Rationality and Modernity* edited by Sam Whimster and Scott Lash (London: Allen and Unwin, 1987), 126. Cited by Verter, 154.

[93] Wasserstrom's discussion of Scholem, Eliade, and Corbin places a large amount of the blame for this turn at their illustrious feet, but the tendency was well-developed before the rise of the discipline of the History of Religions after the Second World War.

[94] Significant works which discuss these religions are: Wade Davis *Passage of Darkness: The Ethnobiology of the Haitian Zombie*, (Chapel Hill NC: University of North Carolina Press, 1988), Maya

looking at the specific form of mysticism expressed through the Great Rite, we can move away from this formulation and see how this ritual and its theology of sexuality can be a viable centre to a modern religion.

First of all, it involves two equal participants, who are defined as Priestess and Priest of the religion. It has a particular form and the set and expectations are defined in the religion – the transubstantiation of the bodies of 'proper persons, properly prepared'[95] into the bodies of the Goddess and Her Consort (in the most usual, heterosexual form, whose language this book will adopt for simplicity's sake – although same sex Great Rite can occur and one of the primary documents drawn upon here is from a lesbian Great Rite).

Although there is a great deal of discussion around issues of sexuality in the neo-Pagan movement and Wiccan movement and a broad acceptance of the polyvariant nature of sexual identity - femininity, masculinity, gay, bisexual, straight, female, male, transgendered and the range of kinks that overlap and cross over them all - and sex magic and the Great Rite exist in a number of variations (more so in some Traditions than others – the feminist Wicca-identified Dianic movement is somewhat heterophobic, anti-male, and transphobic while the most orthodox British Traditional Wiccans tend to be heterosexist and moderately transphobic) this foundation variant is the most common version of the Great Rite ritual and a model for others which serve minority sexual tastes. [96]

Deren *Divine Horsemen: The Living Gods of Haiti* (1953, reprinted Kingston NY: MacPherson and Company, 1988), Robert Farris Thompson, *Flash of the Spirit: African and Afro-American Art and Philosophy* (New York: Vintage/Random House, 1983), and Seth and Ruth Leacock, *Spirits of the Deep: A Study of an Afro-Brazilian Cult* (1972, reprinted New York: Anchor/Doubleday, 1975).

[95] Wiccan phrase meaning a person of the appropriate rank and level of experience and training.

[96] Two valuable sources for discussion of sexual variety are: Hanne

The Priestess and Priest engage in the ritual not for the sake of their own pleasure or to achieve a purely personal enlightenment but to find and bring power and wisdom back into their community. They see the Great Rite as a source of fuel for all the work that they do as clergy, both personally affirming and grounding them and also providing the theological and symbolic foundation to other Wiccan rituals and practices. The experience of the ritual is a powerful affirmation of the panentheism of the Craft and gives personal experience and conviction of the divine nature of each individual.

The Great Rite is linked to other sexual ritual and other sexual activity in Wicca. The use of sexual energy at orgasm and also of sexual fluids to perform magic – to charge talismans, energize spells, and bless marriages - is common in Wicca. The ordinary associations of sex as a source of pleasure, expression of friendship and love and an essential component of relationships of romantic love, is kept in Wicca, although the range of acceptable sexual partners and acts is broadened substantially from that accepted in other religions. These learned associations of sex with love, with relationship, with pleasure, with play, and with shame, guilt and sin, will form a part of the context of

---

Blank, op cit and Olive Skene Johnson's *The Sexual Spectrum: Why We're All Different* (Vancouver: Raincoast, 2007). Examples of serious and effective Pagan kink and sexual minority work includes Pat Califia and Drew Campbell eds *Bitch Goddess: The Spiritual Path of the Dominant Woman* (San Francisco CA: Greenery Press, 1997) and Raven Kaldera ed. *Dark Moon Rising: Pagan BDSM and the Ordeal Path* (Hubbardston MA: Asphodel Press, 2006). There is considerably more Gay and Lesbian work including Christopher Penczak *Gay Witchcraft: Empowering the Tribe* (York Beach ME: Weiser Books, 2003) and Z. Budapest *Feminist Book of Lights and Shadows* (Venice CA: 1976) revised and reprinted as *The Holy Book of Women's Mysteries* (Oakland: Susan B. Anthony Coven , 1979). op cit . From the polyamory community Raven Kaldera *Pagan Polyamory; Becoming a Tribe of Hearts* (Woodbury MN; Llewellyn Worldwide, 2005).

the experience for the actors in the Great Rite, even if
unstated or denied, although the purpose of the ritual is
not directly related to these things.

Wicca emerged as a pro-sex religion at the same
time as the first woman-controlled generally available
birth control method, the Pill, which was distributed by
the National Health Plan in the United Kingdom at a
nominal fee beginning in December 1961, just as the
founder Gerald Gardner's books were being published
(1954, 1959).[97] The separation of sex from reproduction
has theological as well as practical real world
implications that the mainstream religions still are
unable to cope with. Family models need no longer be
based on reproduction only, or on sex, and non-
reproductive sex, such as gay and lesbian sexuality, can
be seen as a basis of lasting families only when
reproduction is by choice. It is also a basic fact of
feminist theory, as well as a practical fact of
heterosexual life, that women cannot be free and equal
until they can control their own reproduction, so the
birth control pill was essential to the lasting second wave
of feminism emerging in the 1960s. The strong linkage
between Wicca and feminism will be demonstrated, and
the centrality of the Great Rite and sexual ritual is an
integral part of that connection.

The attack on sexual ritual by the Patriarchs is
replicated in the anti-pornography and anti-sexuality
faction in the women's movement, which attacks
heterosexuality as inherently oppressive to women, and
which values enforced monogamy just as strongly as the
Patriarchs. The alliance between radical feminists such
as Andrea Dworkin and Katherine McKinnon and the
religious Christian right against pornography was
shocking only to those who do not know the moral
purity origins of much feminism. Dworkin would have

---

[97] Bernard Asbell, *The Pill: A Biography of the Drug that Changed
the World*, (New York: Random House, 1995), 177.

fit in well with the radical feminist moralizers of the late Victorian period, and their essentialism, which granted men sexual agency only to make them bestial and oppressive, and denied women any desire. However, history seems to not be treating the moralizers well.

The Great Rite and *hieros gamos* have been explicitly celebrated in Wicca since the foundation of the religion, and not simply in the most conservative sections of the movement. Deena Metzger's 1985 essay "Revamping the World: On the Return of the Holy Prostitute,"[98] for example, celebrates a rededication to "sexuality and erotic love as spiritual disciplines" and to "re-establish the consciousness of the Sacred Prostitute" as feminist and political activism.[99]

Census data from Canada indicate that Paganism more than trebled in numbers in ten years (a recruitment rate of more than 20% annually) between 1991 and 2001(from 5530 to 21,085), after more than doubling in the previous ten years (2295 to 5530). As 91% of Pagans were native-born Canadians and 89.9% were 15 or older (versus 80.9 and 80.1 for the population as a whole) we grew by conversion in contrast to the other rapidly growing religions like Islam, Hinduism, and Sikhism, religions of immigrants, and despite a strong bias against proselytizing.

Wicca has also brought forward unresolved social issues, mentioned previously. Aside from the intrinsic interest of the new and creative religious expression, therefore, Wicca's growth and influence points to unresolved tensions in the areas which it is addressing and cultural capital which it is producing. Wicca is focused on ritual and experiences derived from

---

[98] Deena Metzger, "Re-Vamping the World: On the Return of the Holy Prostitute," *Heretic's Journal* (Seattle) (Fall 1985), reprinted in *Pagans for Peace* 57 (1992): 6-9.
[99] Ibid, 9.

it rather than theology and so attention must be paid to details of the content of the rituals and the religion. A brief outline of the original forms of their ritual is in the first chapter and a contemporary version in Appendix A. An outline of the ritual of the Great Rite follows. Some of the changes to the ritual and Wiccan practices will be outlined as well – although the form and much of the wording of the foundation rituals remains, there have been changes in them since they were written in the 1940s.

Great Rite ritual script

If the ritual of Great Rite is to be performed the Priestess, after the ritual of Drawing Down the Moon, now seen as embodying the Goddess, will call for the Horned God of the Animals and the Great Hunt, Her Consort, to come into the body of her Priest. Kelly found no version of *Drawing Down the Sun / Horned God* in the original Gardnerian rituals. It remains less common than *Drawing Down the Moon*, because of the Goddess-primary focus of Wicca. There is a version in Janet and Stewart Farrar's *The Witches' Way* (1984).[100]

In it, the Priestess, prior to reciting the Charge of the Goddess, makes the gesture of the Invoking Pentagram of Earth (beginning at top, down to her left, thence up to right, across, down to right, and returning to top)[101] toward the Priest and recites:

Of the Mother darksome and divine / Mine
the scourge, and mine the kiss; / The five-

---

[100] Janet and Stewart Farrar *Witches' Way*, chapter VI, 67-70.
[101] Israel Regardie, *Ceremonial Magic; A guide to the Mechanisms of Ritual* (Wellingborough UK: Aquarian Press, 1980), 124.

point star of love and bliss - / Here I charge you, in this sign.[102]

She then blesses him with the Five-fold Kiss, steps back a pace and recites the invocation:

Deep calls on height, the Goddess on the God / On him who is the flame that quickens her; / That he and she may seize the silver reins / And ride as one the twin-horsed chariot./ Let the hammer strike the anvil, / Let the lightning touch the earth,/ Let the Lance ensoul the Grail,/ Let the magic come to birth.[103]

She then touches with her right forefinger at his throat, left hip, right breast, left breast, right hip, and throat, the Invoking Pentagram of Fire. She spreads her hands, palms forward and continues;

In Her name do I invoke thee / Mighty Father of us all - / Lugh, Pan, Balin, Herne, Cernunnos - / Come in answer to my call! / Descend, I pray thee, in thy servant and priest.[104]

She steps backward and the Priest makes the Invoking Pentagram of Fire toward her while saying "Let there be Light!"[105]

The Great Rite is now most often performed as part of the Third Degree Initiation ritual (the highest grade in the Wiccan initiatory system). Gardner's script as established by Kelly begins with the Priestess binding and then scourging the Priest with three, seven, nine, and

---

[102] Farrar and Farrar *Witches' Way*, 297.
[103] Ibid, 69.
[104] Ibid, 69.
[105] Ibid ,70.

twenty-one strokes separated by short intervals.[106] The Priest is untied, binds the Priestess at the altar and then circumambulates the Circle, proclaiming to the four quarters that the Priestess is prepared and will "proceed to erect the Sacred Altar."[107] He then proceeds to scourge her with three, seven, nine and twenty-one strokes.

The Priestess now is untied and lays down on the altar or floor so that her vagina is at the approximate centre of the circle. The Priest recites an invocation proclaiming that the great altar of the ancients was woman, and that the most sacred point was the centre of the circle, the point of origin which all should adore. He kisses the Priestess' genitals. He invokes "the power of the lifted lance" and touches his genitals.[108]

He recites an invocation, largely taken from the *Gnostic Mass* by Aliester Crowley and at each point marked by a star (*) below, kisses the Priestess' genitals:

> Oh circle of stars (*), whereof our Father is
> but the younger brother (*). Marvel beyond
> imagination, soul of infinite space, before
> whom time is ashamed, the mind
> bewildered and understanding dark, not
> unto thee may we attain unless thine image
> be of love (*). Therefore, by seed and root,
> and stem and bud and leaf and flower and
> fruit do we invoke thee, O, Queen of space,
> O dew of light, O continuous one of the
> Heavens (*). Let it be ever thus, that men
> speak not of Thee as one, but as none, and

---

[106] The scourge is a symbolic cat-of-nine tails whip, typically made with woven cord of embroidery thread. The point of scourging is not to cause pain but to, through rhythmic stimulation, induce a trance state.

[107] Kelly, 60.

[108] This detail comes from Farrar and Farrar *Witches' Way*, 37 although the wording is in Kelly, 60.

let them not speak of thee at all, since thou
art continuous, for thou art the point within
the circle (*), which we adore (*), the fount
of life without which we would not be (*).[109]

He then announces that "in this way truly are
erected the Holy Twin Pillars Boaz and Jachin" and
kisses the breasts of the Priestess.[110] This identifies the
body of the Priestess with the Masonic Temple and her
breasts with the two symbolic pillars of Mercy and
Severity. This particular identification is multi-layered
because the traditional assignment of the Tree of Life in
Ceremonial Magical Kabala is also evoked thereby and
mapped onto the woman's body.

A series of kisses on various parts of her body
are followed by a recitation, again substantially adapted
from the *Gnostic Mass*, but calling upon the God:

secret of secrets that art hidden in the being
of all lives. Not thee do we adore, for that
which adoreth is also thou. Thou art that
and That am I (*). I am the flame that burns
in every man and in the core of every star
(*). I am Life and the giver of Life, and
therefore is the knowledge of me, the
Knowledge of Death (*). I am alone, the
Lord within ourselves whose name is
Mystery of Mysteries (*).[111]

The above invocation formed the foundation to
the Drawing Down the Sun invocations in Janet and
Stewart Farrar, cited above.

---

[109] Ibid, 60-61. This section is adapted slightly from Crowley,
Magick..., 350.
[110] Ibid, 61.
[111] Ibid, 61. This section is adapted slightly from Crowley, *Magick...*,
351.

At this point the Priestess and Priest couple, as the embodiment of the Gods. Both recite together:

Encourage our hearts; Let thy Light
crystallize itself in our blood, fulfilling us
of resurrection. For there is no part of us
that is not of the Gods.[112]

Substantial rewriting of this ritual has occurred in most Wiccan groups that use the Great Rite in Actual, although the pattern established remains constant.

Sacred sexuality and the ritual use of sexual intercourse were highly controversial in the context of late 1940s England, and remain so in the present. However, there was a sex-positive counter-current to Western culture at that time, exemplified by the publication of Alfred Kinsey's *Sexual Behavior in the Human Male* in 1948 and *Sexual Behavior in the Human Female* in 1953, and the publication of *Playboy* magazine, beginning in 1953.

The use of the scourge and of *hieros gamos* is much less common in Wicca today, although they are not unheard of. The Great Rite *In Token*, which was included in the first Book of Shadows in 1949,[113] is very commonly used in public and semi-public rituals of Outer Court Wicca-identified Pagans, which have become frequent occasions for worship. The Great Rite *in Actual* is reserved for coven workings, and most usually only for 3rd Degree Initiations and marriages. As the Wiccan community has grown very rapidly but the number of covens has not grown to keep up with it, the emergence of a group of Outer Court rituals that are based on the Initiatory Mysteries but veil them in

---

[112] Ibid,61. This section is adapted slightly from Crowley, *Magick...*, 352.
[113] Kelly, 67.

symbolism opaque to the non-Initiated has been a pronounced feature of the religion. This process began as early as Chicago's Pagan Way, which was an Outer Court of some Wiccan covens in that city in the early 1970s. The publication of Pagan Way's *A Book of Pagan Rituals* in two volumes in 1974 and 1975 provided a Wicca-based set of simple rituals for non-Initiates. [114]

In the original Great Rite *in Token,* the Priest fills the chalice full of wine and kneels and holds the chalice at about waist level of the Priestess. She holds her athame between her palms, point downward, and inserts the point into the wine, then withdraws it. The Priest recites: "As the Athame is the Male, so the Cup is the female: so, cojoined, they bring blessedness." The Priestess puts her athame aside, drinks and gives the Priest the cup. The Priest then holds up the platen with food on it, Priestess blesses with her athame, then eats and gives food.[115]This is now the most common form of the Great Rite.

The reconstruction of femininity and masculinity in the post-war era with its return to domesticity, the "traditional values of family, home and piety"[116] and the temporary revitalisation of evangelical Christianity runs directly counter to the Wiccan religion in its sexual ethic. However, it would not be correct to see Wicca as an overtly bohemian or counter cultural reaction like the

---

[114] Norman Slater ed., *A Book of Pagan Rituals*, (1974, 1975, republished York Beach ME: Samuel Weiser Incorporated, 1978).
[115] Kelly, 67. A more elaborate version of the blessing wording is frequently used, typically "As the chalice is to the female / So the athame is to the male/ and cojoined they are one in truth / one without the other is incomplete/ for there is no power in all of the world/greater than the power of man and woman/ joined in the bonds of love" (the wording used by the Wiccan Church of Canada, similar to wording found in Farrar and Farrar *Eight Sabbats* op cit 46. The Farrars also give a more elaborate Symbolic Great Rite for Sabbats, 51-53.
[116] Brown, 172.

Beats of the 1950s. The adherents to the first covens were conventional and conservative people in many regards, although there are transgressive and challenging ideas in these first rituals.[117] The one area where the first Wiccans challenged the norms most strongly was in sexual morality, embracing couples living together without marriage, and open relationships with sexual intimacy "regarded as appropriate not only in expressing the mutual love of a committed couple but also close friendships."[118] The stream of occultism from which Wicca emerged was the solidly middle class Golden Dawn, Theosophical movement and Ordo Templi Orientis, not the anarchic or Satanic rebellion of more obscure groups.

An examination of how the religion was first practiced poses several questions and offers inter-textuality for the religion that has evolved; what did Wiccan rituals tell the participants about themselves and their religion, what do they bring to them, and how did their interaction with the material reshape the ritual?

The Goddess is called first in *Drawing Down the Moon*, reflecting the primacy of the Goddess and the Shakti-like view of the Goddess as the energizing, active, creative principle in the Inner Planes, the attractive and evoking principle. Then the Goddess calls in the God through *Drawing Down the Sun,* reflecting the God as Father Earth, material reality to be moulded by the active feminine force. This relationship is also reflected in the Great Rite in Token used in the

---

[117] Philip Heselton, *Wiccan Roots: Gerald Gardner and the Modern Witchcraft Revival*, (Chielveley , UK: Capall Bann Publishing, 2000), gives a detailed portrait of many of Gardner's early associates including Dorothy Clutterbuck, a member of the local gentry, Edith Woodford-Grimes, an English teacher, both of whom were alleged to have served as his mentors and Initiators. Information on other of the early Wiccans can be found in Hutton and Kelly.
[118] Frederic Lamond, *Fifty Years*, 86. When Wicca consisted of one coven, in February1957, Lamond was Initiated into the religion.

consecration of the wine in ritual, as presented by Janet and Stewart Farrar, in which the phallic, active, athame is wielded by the Priestess.[119] In the Farrars' Symbolic Great Rite, however, the athame is wielded by the Priest.[120]

The experience of sacred sex, and other ritual as well, the ecstatic possibility of reclaiming the body and its pleasures from what has hurt, gives Wiccan ritual a therapeutic tone as well as a religious one. This turn toward therapy is particularly pronounced in that feminist wing of Wicca centred on the work of Starhawk and the Reclaiming Tradition of Wicca, a Tradition which draws less directly from Gardner's original rituals than most others.[121] Reclaiming descends from Appalachian folk magic, together with influences from Voodoo and the Hawaiian Huna tradition, although it has been absorbing many Wiccan and New Age ideas as well.[122] Sex magic ritual practiced by Ceremonial Magicians and Reclaiming Witches, among others, is not the Great Rite because it does not necessarily include the aspect of possession trance, an essential component of Great Rite. In the same vein, other sexual magic does not aim to the same ends as Great Rite. It can be performed by Wiccans or others simply as an effective way to raise a great deal of energy to be devoted to healing, job seeking, blessing, or some other magical purposes. There is a minority of Wiccans, now, typically in the British Traditional wing, practicing Great Rite. What is their experience of it?

It is an experience of transubstantiation. The bodies of the Priestess and Priest become the bodies of

---

[119] Janet and Stewart Farrar, *Eight Sabbats* 46
[120] Ibid, 53.
[121] As see, for example Starhawk, *Truth or Dare: Encounters with Power, Authority, and Mystery,* (San Francisco: Harper and Rowe, 1987), which mixes substantial doses of therapy, radical politics and religion all together.
[122] Kelly, 21-22. Kelly here gives a brief sketch of the history of Fairy Tradition, from which Reclaiming Tradition derived.

the Goddess and Her Consort without, however, ceasing to be those of the human servants of the Gods. It is this intermingling of the carnal and the divine, the physical and the metaphysical, that is the key to the emotional and spiritual power of the rite. The sexual act as performed in the *hieros gamos* makes the act sacred, in exactly the same way as the Roman Catholic will see the breaking of bread and drinking of wine as sacred acts during Mass but not at other times. The difference is that the bread and wine are not conscious beings that can experience the transformation and be moved to live their lives differently as a consequence of the transformative mystery. This is why it is typically only Third Degrees that undertake Great Rite, as they are expected to be spiritually mature enough to benefit, and to embody the Gods without fear or expectations.

This rite is symbolic, of course, as are all rituals, which is to say that it is not about the actions which make it up, or at least not only about those things, referring to a more fundamental reality underlying appearances. It is symbolic in this case of the embodiment of the divine, the panentheism central to Wiccan theology, the sacred and holy nature of the body, the sacredness of pleasure and its value as a route to the direct experience of the divine, the idea that the Gods enjoy our bodies as we do, and pleasure as prayer, not as snare. The "Great Rite in token" is thus a symbol of a symbol, removed even further from the thing itself.

The Great Rite challenges on a deep level many of the norms of our society, around pleasure, the nature of the divine, the nature of the body. It directly challenges monogamy, sexual taboos, and body taboos. It is a magickal act and it springs from the power of the Will to desire and to transcend ordinary limits of thought and of action. The universe is malleable, and the Gods can come and play. This is a profound spiritual experience mediated through the most carnal of means, a transubstantiation through an antinomian reclaiming of sex and the body and a rejection of the conventional limits of spirituality.

Although both partners start the ritual in a state of light trance the trance must be intensified throughout until it is Goddess and God, not Priestess and Priest, performing the ritual (PS and P present only enough to be aware, to absorb the energy back into themselves, to be affected by it). There is an energetic feedback in the ritual as experienced – the Goddess yearning for the God and calling Him forth in response to Her desire, the God responding with passion and directness which pulls out a deeper level of desire and so forth. It is the aim of this ritual to attain a transcendent experience beyond the polarity of genders and to give birth within oneself to a mental or spiritual androgyne.[123] The goal is a merger at the point of orgasm which transcends division and which, in an ecstatic feedback, returns and reinforces then dissolves the essence of both sexes.

The structure of a regular ritual is used, although the two celebrants are alone for the Great Rite portion.

Roberto Calosso's discussion of hierogamy and sacrifice in *The Marriage of Cadmus and Harmony* may provide insight into a continuing thread of experience from the Greek model to Wiccan practice. "The appearance of the world came about with the copulation of a god with that which was not god, with the laceration and dispersal of a god's body."[124] Through sex, life, and in life, necessity, the necessity to kill and eat and to experience loss and pain - life constantly is guilty of causing death, a guilt that must be expiated. Hierogamy is akin to sacrifice – offering up, although temporarily,

---

[123] Frater U.D., *Secrets of Western Sex Magic: Magical Energy and Gnostic Trance,*(St. Paul, MN: Llewellyn Publications, 2001), 215.
[124] Roberto Calasso, *The Marriage of Cadmus and Harmony,* translated by Tim Parks, (NY:Knopf, 1993), 293.

one's body and spirit as a gift to the Gods for their use. The parallels between blood and sexual fluids, the equation and connection of life and death, sex and death, eating and sex, all layer underneath the experience of hierogamy.

The fact that humans and gods copulated at the beginning of everything creates a connection between humanity and the divine, a kinship. We share lust, sexual passion, and we can remind ourselves of our fundamental relationship in each sexual act – with orgasm we can project our consciousness back to the primal moment of creation. But this journey back to the beginning is dangerous, and threatens to erase the boundaries between human and divine permanently, to collapse the universe back into primal disorder. So we sacrifice, which reminds both parties of the absolute distinctions of life and death between gods and humans. Sacrifice, however, seen as an aspect of sex, tying life and death together (much as the great story of the maiden Goddess of spring, Persephone, and her *hieros gamos* with the God of death and the underworld, Pluton / Hades, brings sex and death together[125]). Sexual fluids like amrita[126] and semen, being produced and sacrificed from the body, and like blood being tied to life itself, are perfect for this purpose.

Although the Charge of the Goddess says "nor do I demand sacrifice, for behold, I am the Mother of all living and my love is poured out upon the earth,"[127] Wiccans bless food and drink and voluntarily sacrifice a portion as elements in a conversation that they are having with the Gods, an exchange with them that reflects a mutual interest in one another and mutual

---

[125] Ann Suter, *Narcissus* ... op cit Suter's chapter 5, pages 101-117, deals with *hieros gamos* in the stories of Demeter and Persephone.
[126] Literally meaning "the drink which conveys immortality," a term for the female ejaculate.
[127] Farrar and Farrar, *Witches' Way*, 298.

desire of each other. Humans are related to the Gods, although we are constrained by necessity and time as they are not. The occasions when they come to be in time are significant – copulation, bearing our children, eating, pouring libation in imitation of humans as they struggle to understand time and necessity. With libation we say "whatever we do we are this liquid poured away.'"[128]

In the Mystery, for the Great Rite is a Mystery ritual, the Gods are brought into the flesh, into the flesh that decays and dies. "For the initiates, the mysteries are a moment when the gods become tangled with death."[129] Sex is the essential life-giving act, and as the Wiccan Horned God says "I am Life and the giver of Life, and therefore is the knowledge of me, the Knowledge of Death,"[130] because sex opens the gate to death through life.

Although the Great Rite can occur spontaneously, it is expected that at least one party is a "proper person properly prepared" and typically both parties are and they are planning to do the work. In general, the couple must be comfortable with each other and they must be open to the option of sexual ritual (and often they have done sexual ritual together in the past). The Gods must lust after them – they must have a relationship of sexual attraction with at least one deity. In Wicca it is expected that close and personal relationships will emerge between Matron and Patron deities and Their Priestesses and Priests, not always but quite frequently including a quality of sexual attraction. It is also expected that sexual attraction, whether or not it is ever acted upon, will be a part of the energy that works between working partnerships of Priestesses and

---

[128] Calasso, 293.
[129] Ibid, 315-6.
[130] Kelly, 61.

Priests, and to a lesser but real extent among the members of a coven.

The sexual mysticism of the Great Rite takes on a group and social quality under these circumstances, as discussed above. So, although a specific instance of possession trance and ritual sex does not follow the exact ritual form of the Great Rite and may be unexpected it will not come as a complete surprise and will be identified as Great Rite if it fulfils the general expectations for the ritual. The Great Rite is, in other words, not only a specific ritual, but a fundamental mode of engagement with the sacred and sexual that is opened up by the panentheistic idea and the possibility of transubstantiation of the living bodies and spirits of two ritual actors.

The normal form of the Great Rite ritual begins after the usual opening business of a Wiccan ritual – the cleansing, setting aside and consecration of the ritual space, the calling of the directions and the elements, and the welcome of the participants in the ritual.

First-hand accounts of trance and Great Rite

Now, the Goddess is usually Drawn into the Priestess first. She will be in an altered state of consciousness when she draws the God into the Priest. It is usually said that the Priest draws into the Priestess and then the Goddess, acting through the Priestess, calls Her Consort into the Priest. There are occasions where the Priest will have the God drawn into him, first, as in Third Degree Initiation of a Priestess. The experience of the God becoming present in the Priest, as experienced from the Priestess:

> The first time I felt the searing breath of
> Dionysus on my face, I was arrogant
> enough to call the God that cannot be
> commanded into one of our circles... I
> called Dionysus to thank him for His
> encouragement and His inspiration... He
> appeared in my Priest, phallus erect; lips
> parted and stepped into me. He took my
> face in his hands, pressed his Bordeaux
> flavoured mouth to mine and whispered,
> breath hot and gasping, into my ear: "I am
> the one who cannot be commanded. I come
> unbidden. Because you have called me I
> will tell you that I love you and desire you.
> I will ride you, like a horse, to waves of
> ecstasy you have never known..."[131]

The Priestess will have the Goddess drawn into her. The Priest will experience some change in the Priestess as he performs the ritual, unless he is deeply in trance himself at this point. The type of stimulation and the details of the wording of the invocation will change for the Great Rite from the typical coven meeting. The Priestess' typical experience of possession, without the intention of doing Great Rite is:

> I felt Her presence as soon as the
> Invocation began. She was already present
> by the time he finished the Five-Fold Kiss.
> When he began the Invocation, I felt Her
> take me pretty powerfully. I was aware that
> I was rocking back on my heels and could
> barely maintain the concentration to stand.

---

[131] Lady L 3rd, *Dancing with Dionysus*, (unpublished mss. BC, 1997), 1. Those providing first-hand accounts of possession trance and Great Rite will be identified by gender, a letter, their level of Initiation and their general location only. The texts provided are in the possession of the author.

.... I don't recall a lot of it (sign of a good possession). What I remember, more than anything, is the sensation of Her presence, warm and loving and powerful. ... I knew She had something to say... and I stood aside, welcomed Her, and was happy to let her speak.... I lost myself in it. She left almost immediately after She spoke the message.[132]

I have stood in the bow-slinging presence of Artemis and felt Her power and protection at a time when I believed I knew not how to protect myself...I have dripped with the glamour of Aphrodite and felt the amazed and awe-filled heat of the stares placed on me by strangers as I passed them in a grocery store the morning after experiencing Her in a Friday night circle.[133]

In the Great Rite, both Priestess and Priest are possessed by the Goddess and Her Consort. They are in trance and in a ritual space where the usual moral and ethical codes are said to not apply, "a space that is not a space, a time that is not a time"[134]. In this transgressive heterotopia, sex is experienced as a divine force, not merely human, expressed through but not wholly of the body.

There is a feedback loop of sexual stimulation that is needed to raise the bodies to their highest capacity. The repeated invocation and kissing of the Priestess' genitals, type and form of invocations and

---

[132] Lady S 3rd, *June 25/05*, (unpublished mss. BC, 2005), 1. An excerpt from her magickal diary.

[133] Lady L 3rd, op cit, 1.

[134] A typical phrase used in the circle casting, to establish the ritual space as a place set aside from ordinary reality.

specific gestures and the details of coupling are not important. What matters is that at the point of sexual intercourse the Gods are experienced as present and acting through the bodies of the Priestess and Priest, who have stepped aside from their bodies and given them up in ecstasy:

> Herne took over and entered her .It was glorious fucking – pretty well full possession (I felt the horns on my head) and when I came it lasted for a very long time - I was in the pose of Mithras sacrificing the bull, my back arched, mouth open, moaning. Although we had not set out to do Great Rite, we were both being ridden when I was riding her – an incredible sensation. It appears that the Gods had Their minds made up about the matter.[135]

> I felt the presence of both Aphrodite and Morrighan within, each perfectly present, both calling to the God. They called Him and He obeyed. I felt the energy pass between us like a static spark with each kiss, and when I/She kissed His/his mouth, She inspired me to kiss not lightly, but forcefully and passionately, summoning Him forth... I knew the presence of the feral Lord. ... the Horns were huge and [the Priest] was no longer there. ... SHE wanted this keenly and She / They returned powerfully to my body then.[136]

> I was aware the whole time of being both myself and Aphrodite as I was aware that

---

[135] Lord M 3rd, *27th of June 2005*, (unpublished mss. BC, 2005)
[136] Lady S 3rd, op cit, 2.

[she] was both herself and Ares simultaneously. … I was possessed more deeply by Aphrodite and She became playful, kittenish and powerful all at the same time… A mad passionate dance of powerful equals. I wanted to also supplicate to him to bring out his strong protectiveness and strength.[137]

The sacrificed God, the God who dies that we may eat, the God who reduces flesh to soil, the God who thrusts His shoots through the sun-warmed ,moist spring earth... Dionysus had come to me... to initiate me to my third degree. He had come to ride me through the waves of ecstasy. He had come to teach me how to walk the path through ecstasy – not ecstasy of the flesh, but ecstasy of the spirit. … I had been ridden through wave after wave of ecstatic vision.[138]

The after effects of the Great Rite can vary depending on the needs that the person performing it went into it with. It has a powerful and transforming effect, because of its transgressive qualities, the amount of trust and the energy released through letting down one's guard, and the power of directed orgasm. For the Wiccan ritual participants the intention of the Gods in the work, as equal or even dominant actors, which may not be in complete agreement with the intentions of the Priestess or Priest, must be included in the analysis.

---

[137] Lady Sy 3rd, *September 21 2006*, (unpublished mss. BC, 2006), 4-6. Lady Sy's Initiation by Great Rite was lesbian, although her Initiator Drew Down the Sun, and the Rite conformed to the typical Great Rite.

[138] Lady L 3rd, op cit, 4.

We were both a little dazed and needed some time to digest the power of our experience... I have been unabashedly sexual and flirtatious with everyone... AND absolutely fearless of anything. SHE is still with me more than a little. I think they have changed me a bit. I don't think I will ever lose either of these new traits. (Observation a couple of months later – the flirtation has died down but not the sexual confidence or comfort. The fearlessness is not diminished in the least.)[139]

I have danced again with Dionysus ... and I have learned that He is what He is. When He wants what He wants He will come and take it – even if to the receiver of his affections, it feels more like rape than seduction. He is amoral – the most amoral of them all. ... as the teacher of boundaries, some boundaries are permeable and some are iron clad. How you feel about what He does is IRRELEVANT.[140]

The man will be what the woman brings out in him and it is her choice what to do, when to do it, how it will be done etc. He is there to provide the energy. She is there to create with it. I learned that the Gods are grateful for our participation... what I felt was his [Ares'] love for my willingness to be the embodiment of the Goddess and that in me she could play with him.[141]

---

[139] Lady S 3rd, op cit, 3.
[140] Lady L 3rd, op cit, 4.
[141] Lady Sy, op cit, 9-10.

Drawing Down the Moon or the Great Rite are both typically followed by a period of formal or informal debriefing, after the Priestess and Priest have recovered from the state of trance and returned to consensus reality.

This typically takes a few minutes, if possession was strong, and often includes consuming some food and drink. Through the debriefing the ritual participants shape the experience consciously, asking each other for descriptive details of the Gods that possessed their bodies, asking for elaboration on any messages that may have been delivered, and in other ways incorporating the experience into their lives. There is also the strong expectation that every Witch will keep a Book of Shadows, a ritual and magical diary, and will record the details of significant rituals as soon as possible after their performance for future reference, and as a source for intertextual interpretation of future rituals. Although this is a heterotopian time set aside, Wiccan practice takes the insights and energy of the ritual and quickly brings them into the religious life and personal life of participants.

A Sexual Theology

The Great Rite provides a model for ideal sexuality in Wicca – sex that is spiritually informed, ecstatic and deeply connective. It is, however, not a model that is necessarily monogamous, heterosexual, or controlled. It is power, but power that transforms on the shared Wills of both Gods and humans.

Wicca is not centred on the limitation and control of ecstasy, particularly sexual ecstasy, but on trained and wilful expression of it. The rational exploration of magickal subjectivity, a project inherited by Wicca from the Order of the Golden Dawn occultists, as discussed above,[142] continues in an open-ended development here, with libratory prospects and an implicit re-vamping of all of life in mind for both genders. Like all religion, however, it is guided by the spirit, the spirit in the body.

The Great Rite is a central expression of Wiccan spirituality. As Wicca-informed Paganism is becoming more mainstream and less occultist, and as the pressure of a great number of new converts has overwhelmed many teachers, the actual practice has substantially lessened in frequency. Working toward this high degree of trust and release has always taken time and application, and the number of people that have undertaken Great Rite was always small, but the rapid growth and the increasing number of people who come into the religion not proper people, properly prepared, or even near it, has decreased this proportion considerably more.

To what extent can the Great Rite remain a lived reality for practitioners of Wicca and a central symbol, in some form, as the practice becomes increasingly rare? Will the recuperative impulse as expressed in one prominent couple's requirement that participants in the Great Rite "only be a man and a woman between whom intercourse is already a normal and loving part of their relationship: in other words, husband and wife or established lovers"[143] result in the ordinary associations of sex substituting for the esoteric meanings and the loss of intertextual reading against the grain?

---

[142] As see Alex Owen, *Enchantment...* op cit.
[143] Janet Farrar and Stewart Farrar, *Witches' Way*, 32.

Elevating heterosexuality and monogamy to theological absolutes is contrary to the strong norm of free sexual choice in Wicca. It also contradicts the practice of the Gods, generally anything but monogamous and not always heterosexual either, but Wiccans view humans as ethically autonomous, with the Gods as only occasional role models. The critical edge of Wicca on gender and sexuality, and its potential as a spiritual sexually liberating force is in danger of being blunted.

Still, some Wicca-based groups are keeping a strong edge in this area. "The Congregationalist Wiccan Association of British Columbia supports as an article of faith, as stated in the Charge of the Goddess, that "all acts of love and pleasure" are the Goddess' rituals. To us this means that any form of love or sexuality that is non-abusive, and non-coercive, between consenting adults, is acceptable and even desirable. This includes, but is not limited to, relationships that are heterosexual or homosexual, relationships that are monogamous or polyamorous, and relationships that are alternative or conventional." [144]This position led the CWABC to intervene in favour of removing the anti-polygamy laws from Canada's Criminal Code in 2011 when a reference case was put by the province of BC. Their clergy are permitted to perform legal marriages in BC, but are thereby legally prevented from performing marriage like blessings of polyamorous, polyandrous or polygynous families.

Compulsory monogamy is such a deeply entrenched social norm that many sincere Wiccan practitioners must compromise their spiritual impulses in order to preserve their relationships. If the circumstances of someone's life, individual psychology or relationships do not permit a completely pragmatic approach to Great

---

[144] From the CWABC website www.cwabc.org accessed 10:44 pm, February 26th 2012.

Rite, the norm need not be elevated into a religious principle in contradiction to Wicca's foundation principles. Acknowledging the central importance of the Great Rite does not make its performance obligatory. A Priestess or Priest who practiced Great Rite indiscriminately would be going counter to the spirit of it. The power of a conscious choice of what a Priest/ess will do ritually is as significant in this regard as in any other.

Once experienced the Great Rite provides the bedrock of certainty that informs the rest of life. But as a Mystery, it must be experienced, not just described, before some of the energy and insights can continue to act in other ritual and non-ritual contexts. One can recall the experience and work with the energy through masturbation or while doing the Great Rite in Token in coven or other ritual.

The amount of preparatory work required and the elitism in the requirements for sexual, emotional and spiritual maturity, prior to that, given the populism in modern Wicca-influenced neo-Paganism, has led to many undervaluing or disregarding the actual Great Rite. Symbolic or solo sex magick or Great Rite in Token is not enough alone although sex magic is mostly practiced solo. As sex magician and author Frater U.D. puts it: "Sex-magical partner workings are not quite the exception, but autoerotic practices are certainly the rule."[145] By many would-be Priest/esses denying the centrality of the Rite, because they have not done it, and are unprepared to attempt it, or are afraid to challenge social norms in order to attempt it, the religion is weakened.

Wiccans are acting "as if" they believe, to see what the results are, in search of experiences which are valuable to them, rather than in search of confirmation to

---

[145] Frater U.D., 142

absolute belief statements. They are not performing an intellectual dodge to make their religion non-falsifiable, but understanding the playful possibility of ritual and magical exploration and the positive results in aesthetic and psychological happiness that result from a rational subjectivity in the exploration of the spiritual. By developing on the bases of the original practices of the religion, Wicca's challenge to the hegemony of Christian values has continued. The new aspects of its religious discourse about sexuality, which the gay and lesbian, polyamorous and 'lifestyle' community members now involved have added indicates that it continues as a heterotopia, and continues to generate new religious compensators and spiritual capital for its members.

To continue to accumulate cultural capital for its members and to be effective in the world in building toward social transformation in tune with its values, the Wiccan religion must continue to resist the normalizing impulse and to shape its development on the basis of these values. As the next generation grows up in the religion, they will shape it, increasingly (although a majority of Wiccans will continue to be converts).

Part of the challenge facing Wicca is how to reawaken the critique of Patriarchal sexual limits, in a situation where the religion is growing rapidly and is, particularly, adding young families and children. What alternatives can Wicca develop? The structural adjustment in some communities of an Inner Court for clergy and Initiates, Outer Court for the regular congregants, and the broader Sabbat congregation for the laity may be one useful option. What viable alternatives exist to the nuclear family? How can Wiccans avoid setting up a counter-morality that limits people's choices just as badly as compulsory heteromonogamy does? The argument has been made, among others by Rodney Stark and William Bainbridge, that sectarian movements necessarily move toward the mean and normalize their practices.

It is not the choice of monogamy that threatens the Great Rite, because it can be, and often is in some form, a practice of committed Wiccan couples, but the lack of understanding of its central importance to the religion as a whole. The inadequate critique of the Patriarchal sexual limits which leads those Wiccan traditions that embrace the use of the ritual to often endorse compulsory heterosexuality and only monogamy in its performance weakens the Craft. Those sexual minorities that are growing in the religion feel disenfranchised by this.

The development of Wicca points to the possibility of a religious embrace of sexuality and of sexual variety in a way that does not simply *tolerate* sexual variety (thus implicitly privileging one expression above the others) but which builds a workable theology around the differences and common thread in ecstasy. It also demonstrates that sexual ecstasy and religious ecstasy can be mutually reinforcing, and that a pro-sex feminist-informed spirituality is workable. Although the long-term viability of the Wiccan sexual spirituality is an open question the success thus far in building a religion embracing sexual variety and free expression poses a substantial challenge to the less sex-positive theologies of other religions, and the separation of the (sexual) body and spirit, central to the secular outlook as well as mainstream (Christian) religion.

The Uses of Ecstasy: Ritual and Practical Mysticism in Wicca

*"Ritual is a means of performing the
way things ought to be in conscious
tension to the way things are in such a
way that this ritualized perfection is
recollected in the ordinary,
uncontrolled, course of things." –*
Jonathan Z. Smith [146]

This chapter discusses ritual preparation for the experience of mystical states in the Wiccan religion, explanations applied to each stage of the training, and practical consequences and ritual expressions that flow from these experiences into the religion as a whole. It begins with an overview of Wicca and associated neo-Pagan religions, moves through some theories of ritual and mystical trance experiences, in particular the cognitive theory of Harvey Whitehouse and Victor Turner's discussion of liminality and *communitas*[147]. We then explorr the training toward trance expertise in Wicca and some of the expertise and knowledge required of Wiccan ritual specialists, stages of trance, an analysis of the most common ritual used to trigger trance (Drawing Down the Moon and Sun), then public (Outer Court[148]) derivatives from that experience. Finally it

---

[146] Jonathan Z. Smith *Imagining Religion: from Babylon to Jonestown* (Chicago: University of Chicago Press, 1982), 63.
[147] Harvey Whitehouse *Modes of Religiosity: A Cognitive Theory of Religious Transmission* (Walnut Creek: AltaMira Press, 2004); Victor Turner *The Ritual Process: Structure and Anti-Structure* (1969, New Brunswick NJ: Aldine Transaction Publishers, 2007). "Liminality" means "on the threshold" and this refers to rites of passage specifically, but also to the "in between the worlds" assignment of ritual space in Wicca, and to ritual ambiguities. "Communitas" refers to a state of equality, a generalized social bond that underpins all of the hierarchic or differentiated structures of society. Turner, 94-97.
[148] "Inner Court" /"Outer Court" – in Wicca the Inner Court is the private coven scale ritual and mystical knowledge available to Initiates only, while Outer Court is public or semi-public community

looks at the hoped-for embedding of spiritual capital[149] generated through mystical experience into the religion as a whole, and evaluates this blending of Imagistic and Doctrinal religion.

Wicca is an initiatory mystery religion of clergy that was founded in the United Kingdom in the late 1940s by a group of occultists led by Gerald Gardner and his Priestesses, most notably Dafo (Edith Grimes-Stafford) and Ameth (Doreen Valiente / Vlachopoulos). It grew out of an occult milieu and its influences can be traced back several hundred years – good histories of this milieu and of Wicca are Joscelyn Godwin's *Theosophical Enlightenment*[150] and Ronald Hutton's *Triumph of the Moon*[151]. It was substantially based on ideas and ritual of the *Ordo Templi Orientis* and Order of the Golden Dawn ceremonial magic groups, fragments of British folklore and the writing of Margaret Murray and Geoffrey Leland.[152] There is a cluster of neo-Pagan religions that derive from roughly the same sources, or from Gardner's groups, and all call themselves Wiccan. This book uses a conservative definition of Wicca – those groups in the broadly "British Traditional" stream, that are most similar to the original Wiccan religion, and the public groups influenced directly and led by Initiates into them. This conservative faction represents what is uniquely and most typically Wiccan in its approach to blending ritual and trance.

Wiccans view mystical experience as an essential part of clergy training and expect their highest

---

ritual or the exoteric discussion of the esoteric experiences. Covens are private worship and magical groups, typically no more than five or six members in size.

[149] The concept of 'spiritual capital' that I have used throughout this book is derived from Bradford Verter, "Spiritual Capital..." op cit.

[150] Joscelyn Godwin *The Theosophical Enlightenment* ... op cit.

[151] Ronald Hutton *Triumph* ... op cit.

[152] Aidan A. Kelly *Crafting* ....

level clergy to undergo trance experiences on a regular basis. They see mystical experience as providing energy and correction to all else that happens in the religion, and the ritual and institutions that contain and provide meaning to these experiences as creating a great deal of spiritual capital. Wiccans do not view the mystical as inexplicable but work rationally to train individuals that are recognized as talented in trance states to undergo these experiences on behalf of the entire community.

It is not a question of belief but of experience – Wiccans do not have a credo. Their intention is to produce a religion of prophets, with direct access to the Gods, using symbols, including images and beliefs, as tools. They assume the capacity to connect directly with divinity, the possibility of meaning, and that experiences are the foundation of everything, not ideas. In this they can refer to William James' pragmatism[153] and lay claim to be materialist mystics.

Wicca is an elitist religion that most people are not suited to. Belief is not enough alone, it takes Talent[154] and the capacity to experience certain things and to go through a process of personal transformation, Initiation, before one can practice Wicca. It also is not a solo path, but one where the most profound experiences are the result of group efforts. The experience of *communitas* (after Victor Turner) and the ecstatic trance is found in small group, coven, practice but is ideologically applied to more public ritual as well because of the view of the religion as a community. The term 'community' is usually applied by Wiccans to the whole religious movement across the spectrum of factional differences.[155]

---

[153] William James *Varieties* ... op cit.
[154] "Talent" is used here in the folk meaning of a psychic ability out of the ordinary.
[155] Victor Turner *The Ritual Process* op cit 94-165.

The small-group coven form is highly preferable in Wiccan practice because of the capacity of a group of trained people to focus their energy magically, the development and nurturance of an egregore[156], the difficulty of establishing the level of trust needed and the strength of ecstatic trance induction done by experienced people, the sophistication of an informed discussion of the Gods and the direct revelation from the Gods through possession and inspiration trance, the aesthetic pleasures of well-constructed and performed ritual, for these and other reasons. However, implicit in this is that the coven is not able to tolerate free-riders and uncommitted dabblers – it is for participants, not spectators, a leader-full group rather than a simple hierarchy. Covens are rare, although normative in the Wicca-identified movement, and only a minority of Wicca-identified Pagans belong to one. For less committed participants in the Wiccan-influenced religions, public and semi-public groups led by Wiccan clergy (Outer Court) have existed since at least the early 1970s, when Chicago's Pagan Way group was founded to "create a Pagan society" and "to build our temples in the towns…"[157]

Ritual is enacted and experiential – not a literary form but performative[158]. Mysticism is first experiential, with meanings implicit and indirect, with overt meanings and interpretations derived or applied later. The two

---

[156] This is a group mind / guardian spirit that comes into existence when a group of people engage in a common project. Magical groups often deliberately intensify the symbolism and importance of this idea and use the group mind as a reservoir for group identity and energy and a common store of symbolism.

[157] Herman Slater ed. *A Book of Pagan Rituals* op cit, 3-4.

[158] "Performative" not only in the sense of being a 'performance' but also in the sense of being actions that cause effects in and of themselves – for example as the ritual statement "I now pronounce you married" in a wedding ceremony is a performative statement or the frequent closing statement of a magickal spell in Wicca, "As I say it, so mote it be."

seem to have intuitive connections, in particular as a person is "in flow" in either an effective ritual or mystical state, although there is the Romantic argument that ritual (as "mere formalism") contradicts the gifts of the spirit. Making the connections between mystical experience and ritual competence in clergy active and overt and ensuring that ritual experiences are informed by mystical experience, as Wiccan Temples do, challenges the argument that these are two incompatible areas of experience with different rules.

Meanings that are assigned to mystical experiences, like those of ritual performances, reflect the cultural and religious predispositions of the person having the experience or participating in the ritual, not anything inherent to it. The technical aspects of trance induction and ritual performance are, however, typically taught in a context of assigned meanings. Facets of this relationship between mystical and ritual experience, context, and meaning are addressed in theories of ritual and religion, but each theory is partial – dealing with issues of power, death and rebirth, social structures or some other part of the synergy. Scholarly approaches that deal only with the application of the mystical, not the thing itself, or those that reduce the experience to a matter of personal psychology cannot account for its social potency, while those scholars that accept the explanations offered by the mystic as sufficient are misled into another blind alley.

The Wiccan approach to mystical training fits well within the pragmatic and practical approaches of Abraham Maslow and William James, previously referred to. Maslow's cross-cultural and materialist description of the typical features of the mystical state in *Religions, Values and Peak Experiences*[159] affirms the mystical (Peak) experience as a common and deeply

---

[159] Abraham H. Maslow, *Religions, Values, and Peak Experiences*, op cit.

meaningful human capacity with qualities as a pure experience that are described in similar ways cross-culturally. Commonly there is the perception of the universe as an integrated and unified whole in which the perceiver has a place and all belongs there, that the other things of the universe have purposes and meanings separate from human needs and meanings, that the world is only beautiful, good and worthwhile. [160] Values typically extracted from the experience and applied to the fundamental nature of reality include truth, goodness, beauty, wholeness, aliveness, the transcendence of differences, perfection, necessity, justice and others[161]. The difference between a mystic's and an idealist's understanding is that the mystic has had direct experience of the truth of these ideals and is acting from knowledge rather than faith or hope. This knowledge is subjective and needs to be tested against reality, as typically experienced, and tempered by organization, to produce spiritual capital and cultural force.

William James, cited earlier, in *Varieties of Religious Experience* speaks of mystical experiences as 'meaning-making' or 'meaning-provoking' and not inherently meaningful. He sets reasonable limits to the authority of the mystical state and argues that it must be tested by the same empirical methods that would be used to evaluate any other experience. Wicca explicitly tests the authority of mystical states and the prophetic revelations of its clergy, both as a regular debriefing in the private small group context in which trance experiences typically occur and in community discussion.

By stating that mystical experience provokes meaning-making activity rather than containing meaning in itself, this book does not discount the truth or

---

[160] ibid, 59-68.
[161] ibid, 91-94.

meaningfulness of any mystical experience or the ritual and religious expressions of the truths derived from it. As part of the ancient quarrel between fact and meaning the author firmly agrees with both sides, with the caveat that meanings are provisional and derivative, that religion resembles art and not science, and that there must be several correct explanations of the same fact depending on the frame of reference. The frame of reference that is applied here accepts that mystical experiences are positive and to be sought after, that they point toward a deeper underlying spiritual structure to the universe and to human life, and that they transform the people experiencing them in ways that are not completely within their control. This book also explicitly accepts the validity and usefulness of the Wiccan spiritual path, without presuming anything about other spiritual paths.

The details of interpretation and symbolism do not exhaust the experience, but shape it and partially tame it. As Alfred Korzybski put it: "A map is not the territory it represents, but, if correct, it has a similar structure to the territory, that accounts for its usefulness,"[162] and to the extent that the explanations or meanings applied to a mystical experience conform to its impact on the person having it (with the important caveat that the context partly determines what experiences are possible), or, most crucially for this book, to the extent that the ritual of trance induction reliably produces trance and the interpretations produce spiritual capital for the religion, then we may act as if the explanation is true because it is useful. The balance of mystical Inner Court experience and the Outer Court ritual expression, the ineffable meaning-making and the (provisional) meanings derived from it and brought

---

[162] Alfred Korzybski *Science and Sanity: An Introduction to Non-Aristotelian Systems and General Semantics* (1933, Lakeville, Conn. : International Non-Aristotelian Library Pub. Co.1958 4th edition), 38.

forward for the uninitiated laity in the Wiccan religion, is dynamic and ever-shifting but fruitful.

Experiences emerge out of a context of preparation and expectation, not sui generis but also not wholly determined by the context. The setting of expectations, the preparation to become a "proper person, properly prepared"[163] can be quite lengthy and involve a number of exercises and pieces of knowledge. The thing itself, the mystical experience, develops and grows, as we shall see below, through a number of stages before we arrive at the goal of enlightenment or, in the Wiccan context, full-scale trance and possession in ecstasy.

Harvey Whitehouse and "modes of religiosity"

After Harvey Whitehouse,[164] ritual in religion is used to transmit complex theological notions beyond the intuitively obvious personal revelations - the stories, truth statements and meaning statements at the centre of the religions. It is a vehicle for the preservation and growth of spiritual capital in other words. He divides ritual into the Doctrinal and Imagistic modes – the long and slow osmosis of the Doctrinal mode that "codifies revelations into a logically coherent linguistically transmitted body of doctrines… frequent repetition … leaders … orthodoxy" [165] with a focus on homilies and emotionally cool repetition and the intense and deep

---

[163] Wiccan phrase meaning a person of the appropriate rank and level of experience and training.
[164] Harvey Whitehouse in *Modes of Religiosity* op cit.
[165] Theodore Vial "Teaching the Cognitive Approach" from *Teaching Ritual* ed. Catherine Bell (Oxford: American Academy of Religion/Oxford University Press, 2007), 166

Imagistic mode that "tends to transmit revelation through sporadic collective action, using 'multivocal iconic imagery'"[166] and is anything but cool. The first consolidates and the other energizes (and sometimes destroys). "The advantage of the imagistic mode is that it sustains both memory and motivation: its disadvantage is that it forms only small, closely knit groups. Though the doctrinal mode is easily transported and can form large anonymous communities, it seems not to be sustainable by itself over the long term. Large, successful traditions, then, will have some pattern of interaction of the two modes."[167]

In some religious traditions this potential synergy is not considered – the more formalistic and Doctrinal traditions separate out and often suppress the ecstatic (to their detriment), while many mystical and magical groups effloresce and die without offspring because of a refusal to temper the Imagistic approach to the needs of the uninitiated. This book considers some Wiccan traditions' wilful and explicit melding of the two modes of religious experience through paired Inner Court and Outer Court structures. Wicca began in the late 1940s purely as an initiatory mystery tradition of clergy working in small closed groups (covens) and this path remains at the centre of the Wiccan movement.

Whitehouse' third mode of religiosity – the intuitively satisfying folk religious expressions - provides a foundation to the experience of the more complex rituals layered on top of it. Because Whitehouse does not see the intuitively satisfying and spontaneous folk traditions as providing meaningful or complex religious ideas and engagement, and because they do not need to be committed to memory and his initial interest is in memory encoding not theology or ritual per se, he spends very little time discussing them.

---

[166] Vial, op cit, 166.
[167]Vial, op cit, 167.

In Wicca these folk religious beliefs and practices are taught as foundations to the more complex later developments, and the tension between lay/folk and clergy/ Imagistic and Doctrinal expression are reduced. Ritual borrows back and forth among all three modes (as it does in other religions, but explicitly in Wicca).

The ecstatic and Initiatory path is definitely Imagistic and necessarily so. By incorporating the idea that raw experience needs to be cooked by service to the community to fully nourish the soul into the coven practices[168], a means of resolving the tension between the two modes and bringing the spiritual fire of the Imagistic into the Doctrinal has been arrived at, and through incorporating the folk religion, the stages of religious knowledge acquisition have been opened up to even less committed practitioners. The pragmatic shift away from exegesis to practice, a consequence of the emphasis on magick and performative ritual, also marks the Wiccan paths. The Inner and Outer Court structures that some Wiccan groups have built reflect both the clergy's need to complete the integration of these experiences and the need of the non-clergy adherents to Wicca to transform the mystical into cultural/spiritual capital to the benefit of all Wicca-identified Pagans.

Ritual thoughts

The largest part of the Wicca-identified Pagan movement's adherents has no direct experience with ecstatic trance or mystical experience. They are the equivalent of the laity of any religion, attending rituals, providing some degree of support for community

---

[168] A formulation taken from Claude Levis-Strauss *The Raw and the Cooked: Mythologiques, Volume 1* trans. John Weightman and Doreen Weightman (1969, Chicago: University Of Chicago Press, 1983)

institutions, consulting the Priestesses and Priests around crises and for rites of passage.

Because formal institutions and organized bodies are rare in the neo-Pagan movement, these people's first ritual experience is likely to have been a seasonal celebration whose ritual text was cribbed directly from a prominent author's book of seasonal rituals, performed by an ad-hoc Priestess or Priest with a minimum of formal training or experience herself. However, the authors, and many of the community leaders, generally have had these experiences, and there is an increasing movement in the religion to return to the mystical centre and also to develop institutions to formalize training and to link clergy more directly with the broader lay community of Wicca-identified neo-Pagans.

What is being described in this book is, therefore, a work in progress as the Wiccan religion continues to adapt to very rapid growth, growth that has outstripped the capacity of the established Initiatory framework and the training process for clergy in an Initiatory Mystery Tradition and that presents the problem of preserving the mystical core and spreading the insights from mystical experience out to the majority of non-Initiated. We can observe a Doctrinal tradition taking shape from necessity in Wicca-identified Paganism and get a clearer understanding of social factors that lead to this development.

Ritual produces predispositions toward particular types of triggering experiences but does not point toward any necessary meaning or interpretation. How to most effectively obtain the state of trance and suggestibility, and to reinforce, through suggestion, the meanings that the religious leaders want people to derive from their mystical experiences involves a conscious construction of habitus (après Bourdieu) through choice and not tradition. This also immediately points toward the kind of questions about power that Foucault poses[169] – who decides that meanings to construct, who benefits from them, and what are the longer term consequences of these power relations? What relationships of resistance are also embedded in the ritual styles and performance and the meaning-assignment and meaning-making? Is Wicca co-created or elite manipulated? *Communitas* is, to some degree, a dodge around these issues of power, and is understood and used that way often by leaders in the Wiccan religion.

The ideological identification of Wiccans with peasantry, women, and other subaltern[170] groups in European history and conquered peoples like the Scots and Irish, also places the Witches in the direct line with Turner's understanding of *communitas* and *liminality*: "*Communitas* breaks in through the interstices of structure, in *liminality;* at the edges of structure, in marginality; and from beneath structure, in inferiority."[171] The class base of Wicca is largely middle-class, as is true with most new religions, but its origin myth is as the religion of the subalterns, derived from Leland's *Aradia: Gospel of the Witches* and Margaret Murray's *Witchcult in Western Europe*, strong influences on the original coven, and reinforced in the later 1960s with the

---

[169] For example in Michel Foucault *The Archaeology of Knowledge and The Discourse on Language* translated by A. M. Sheridan Smith (1971, New York Pantheon/Random House, 1972), chapter 4 "The Formation of Enunciative Modalities", pages 50-55

[170] "Subaltern" is a term adopted by Antonio Gramsci to refer to those groups in society who are subject to the hegemony of the ruling classes. After Gramsci, the Subaltern Studies group of historians promoted the term and the approach to multiple-view-pointed histories of suppressed classes and groups of people, initially in South Asia, with the key feature being the resistance to elite domination. See Bill Ashcroft, Gareth Griffiths and Helen Tiffin *Post-Colonial Studies: The Key Concepts* (London: Routledge, 2000), 215-219.

[171] Turner, op cit, 128.

counterculture and feminist movements' discovery of Wicca.[172]

 With the factional divisions in the Wicca-identified neo-Pagan movement alluded to above and the differences around whether and in what way to organize Outer Court public or semi-public Temples or ritual circles, the questions of power are pressing. Because of a strong norm of 'leaderless' non-hierarchic and consensus based decision-making in the most feminist-influenced wing of the movement, leadership in which faction is exercised covertly and through groups of friends rather than through leadership accountable to the members[173] and in most cases Outer Court structures in other parts of the movement are client cults centred around one or two strong personalities rather than formal organizations with accountable leadership. However, ecstatic trance is rarely practiced in the non-hierarchic faction, and the client cult leaders, if they are effective, will have the same dynamic around ecstatic insight and ritual as the specific fraction of the movement, the Temple-centred more-or-less church-like Outer Courts working with a substantially British Traditional Inner Court core, that this book is dealing with, so they need not be discussed separately for our purposes.

 Wiccan Inner Court ritual establishes the ritual space as a heterotopia, as in Foucault's discussion of the term as a space set aside for the intensification of cultural differences, conflicts or social options. Heterotopian sanctuaries allow the focused development and working out of social facts and may or may not later be reintegrated into society as a whole as catalysts for social change. [174] The heterotopian quality is qualified

---

[172] Leland's *Aradia:* op cit Margaret Murray *Witchcult in Western Europe* (Oxford: Oxford U. Press, 1921)

[173] Jo Freeman *The Tyranny of Structurelessness* (1970, reprinted Montreal: Bevy of Anarchist Feminists, 1986)

[174] Michel Foucault , "Of Other Spaces" 22-27.

by the degree of social tolerance - those rituals that most resemble and reinforce normal social roles and power distributions are least heterotopian (and least challenging or productive of specifically Wiccan spiritual capital). It also is a liminal space (after Turner) with participants in between states, and outside of their conventional social roles.[175] Outer Court rituals, although much less transgressive, follow the same form and general pattern in their performance and so allude to the heterotopian qualities of Inner Court. They are made a stage between mundane life and the ecstatic by this mirroring.

The Wiccan view, usually implicit, is that ritual is practice, not theory, and not dogma. However, consistent and coherent ritual experimentation and goal-directed ritual construction is limited where the theoretical dimension has not been addressed. After Marx' *Theses on Feuerbach* , "[we] must prove the truth, that is, the reality and power, the this-sidedness of [our] thinking in practice. The dispute over the reality or non-reality of thinking that is isolated from practice is a purely *scholastic* question."[176] We are faced with a practical or technical question here, then – not a theological, moral, or ethical issue but much more concrete – not "what is right?" but "what works?" and again, as per Marx, seeing that "the religious sentiment is itself a social product and ... the abstract individual ... belongs in reality to a particular form of society,"[177] and concerning the most effectively integrating these experiences into the whole religion and the broader society.

Although there is a minority of Wiccans who adhere very firmly to the rituals handed down from the founders of the religion (in contradiction to the founders' own enthusiastic bricolage, adaptation and mimicry) it is

---

[175] Victor Turner, *Ritual Process*, chapter 3, 94-130.
[176] Karl Marx "Theses…", 144.
[177] ibid, 145

a norm in the religion that clergy, initiates, must write rituals inspired by their personal connection to the Gods. The conscious creation and adaptation of ritual, as a matter of course, creates fluid and very pragmatic use of it as a tool for spiritual exploration that actively subverts dogmatism. The Wiccan community is comfortable with aesthetic judgement of the value of a particular piece of liturgy. Although ritual is not seen as simply artwork (in the 'art for its own sake' mode) it is seen as legitimate to pay attention to language, pacing, movement and gesture, and the theatrical tricks as well as the theological content of a piece of ritual.

After Aiden Kelly and William James, this book embraces the use of artistic criteria to evaluate the Wiccan religion. There is good and bad art, and good and bad religion, quite aside from any moral criteria. As Kelly said, "If a new ritual works better for some people than the old one did, if it gives them a religious experience or dimension they had been lacking, then it represents a step in the right direction, and is a gift of the spirit."[178] This book agrees with Kelly that Wicca is an important new religion, in part because of its emphasis on creativity and adaptation, and also because of the strong integration of mystical experience into the general ritual and practice of the community, both clergy and laity. In addition, the particular forms of ritual and ecstatic practice chosen are significant for their resistance to the powers that be – in Wicca very definitely the attitudes to sexuality, particularly the strong affirmation of minority sexualities, the affirmation of the power and worth of nature, the use of magic and the power of women, are framed in ways that challenge the norms. Bricolage in Wiccan ritual includes the resisting elements of mocking mimicry as well as (even in conjunction with) the admiring side, so it is

---

[178] Aiden Kelly *Crafting* 181. James *Varieties…* provides valuable points to illuminate the aesthetic appeal of religion on pages 395-398.

self-critical (although less so than the Zuni, for one
example).

Ritual action can allude to the mystical and can
induce mystical and trance states because it necessarily
"involves an interplay of congruous and incongruous
frames of reference." Ritual efficacy requires this
interplay[179] between the ecstatic and the mundane,
expressing the immanent and transcendent qualities of
deity. This play of incongruity is sacramental action that
transforms the ordinary from one reality to another while
at the same time retaining the original state of
ordinariness. Ritual tells us something about ordinary
matter and substance as they transform it.[180] Michael
Taussig speaks of the profane and sacred as constitutive
of one another – the capacity to be defiled meaning
sacred, of being purified marking the profane, binary
oppositions becoming inseparable and the requirement
of one another.[181] The sacred does not exist without the
profane or the profane without the sacred. It is the
making sacred (sacramental) quality of ritual and its
mimetic and constitutive powers that make it worth
doing, and central to religion.

Another valuable viewpoint on the
sacred/profane interplay and power issues, Thomas
Moore's *Dark Eros*, looks at the Marquis de Sade and
his writing and philosophy as religious writing. Sade
desires the power to degrade and despoil - the
sacred/profane dichotomy with the sacramental and
desacramental being both strong needs of the soul - to
"make sacred" and to "make profane." Moore is
interested in what Sade tells us about non-consensual

---

[179] Richard A Gardner "Reflections on Ritual in Noh and Kyogen"
from *Teaching Ritual* ed. Catherine Bell op cit, 225.
[180] Linda Ekstrom and Richard D. Hecht "Ritual Performance and
Ritual Practice: Teaching the Multiple Forma and Dimensions of
Ritual" from *Teaching Ritual* ed. Catherine Bell op cit, 234-5.
[181] Michael Taussig *Defacement: Public Secrecy and the Labor of the
Negative* (Stanford CA: Stanford U. Press, 1999) 52-3.

degradation and what our desire for it (both to inflict and to experience) reveals about this interplay between sacred and profane and the healthy soul (that in his opinion is NOT the pristine soul but the experienced and redeemed soul).[182] The frequent rituals of death and dismemberment, the pain and fear often included in initiation rituals, fit well into Moore's discussion, and Wiccan trance and Initiation rituals involve symbolic ego-death and the transcendent loss of innocence. The recent and growing influence of the kink communities[183] into Wicca has produced some valuable ritual work and thought explicitly using these darker elements – the Dark Mother and the destructive/creative parts of the divine, although these are minority interests.[184]

And further, by recognizing that many of the questions of religion are universal problems and that the principal means of working out religious problems has been through ritualization, borrowing and adapting ritual elements from other contexts is a reasonable, and efficacious, means of addressing issues. It introduces both congruity, through dealing with the same issues, and incongruity, by the cognitive dissonance of introducing these elements that may not fit well together on the surface.

Some of the Subaltern Studies school of post-colonial historians have produced useful work in this vein, for example Dipesh Chakrabarty, mentioned earlier, and Homi Bhabha.[185] This estrangement can also

---

[182] Thomas Moore *Dark Eros: The Imagination of Sadism* (Woodstock CT: Spring Publications, 1990,1994).
[183] "Kink communities" are the sexual minority communities centred on sado-masochism, bondage, and fetishistic sexual interests and role-playing that satisfies these needs. In many cities there are regular kink events, parties and club nights that cater to these communities.
[184] Examples of serious and effective work in this vein include: Pat Califia and Drew Campbell eds *Bitch Goddess* op cit and Raven Kaldera ed. *Dark Moon Rising* op cit.
[185] Dipesh Chakrabarty *Provincializing Europe…* op cit in particular

give valuable new insights into things that we have taken for granted. We can see subaltern points of view – like the mystical trance understanding of Wiccan practitioners - as ordering points for action, without needing to explain them by means of some other theoretical framework. Accepting multiple voices and the legitimacy of religious perspectives is essential for this book's analysis and "hierarchic claims to the inherent originality or 'purity' of cultures are untenable … the meaning and symbols of culture have no primordial unity or fixity; that even the same signs can be appropriated, translated, rehistoricized and read anew."[186]

Ritual practices and exercises are embodiments – making the actions part of the body's normal functioning, allowing them to be felt in and through the body. Theory is constructed as human bodies in action – we create our own theories of ritual as we do ritual.[187] The key is doing and thereby acquiring the skills of ritualization that permit the ritual agent to effectively create a ritualized space and interact effectively with the powers of the spirit, whether Gods or forces of nature.[188] And the fundamental framework of ideas should, after Lakoff's philosophy of the embodied mind, be recognized as categories of the body – it is the embodied mind and the mindful body that creates ritual and experiences ecstatic trance, not a viewpoint soul apart from the body.[189] So the ritualization of mystical

---

his chapters 3 'Translating Life Worlds into Labor and History' and 4 'Minority Histories, Subaltern Pasts,' 72-113. Homi K. Bhabha *The Location of Culture* (London: Routledge, 1994), in particular his discussion of hybridity.

[186] Bhabha 37-38.

[187] Mary E. McGann "Teaching Rites Ritually" from *Teaching Ritual* ed. Catherine Bell op cit, 147-160.

[188] Catherine Bell, *Ritual Theory, Ritual Practice,* op cit and *Ritual: Perspectives and Dimensions* (Oxford: Oxford University Press, 1997), 81-2.

[189] George Lakoff and Mark Johnson *Philosophy in the Flesh: The*

experiences embodies them and fixes their insights, to a degree, in the bodies of those that perform the rituals, even the non-Initiated and non-mystics. And now this book's discussion needs to move from the theoretical to the practical, toward the embodiment and training for it.

Theological and Practical Details of Wiccan Clergy Training.

Without sacrificing intellectual standards, there is an obligation on those teaching clergy to assist their students to become better, more whole, more complete people. A person who gives blood regularly, who volunteers in her community, who appreciates and creates art of some sort, who has developed his spiritual and ethical understanding, is closer to the ideal. These things make one a richer and more interesting person. They also prepare one as a mentor, not just an authority, and ground the spiritual work aesthetically and practically.

The essence of the sense of community and communion with the divine together with one's fellows in human community (or, after Turner, *communitas*)[190] that is fundamental to Wiccan engagement can be summarized in the four principles of Trust, Open-ness, Realization, and Interdependence (TORI principles). Wiccan rituals, particularly those in the Inner Court, are shaped by those four fundamental ideas, implicitly or explicitly. This particular phrasing and system comes from Pagans for Peace Tradition of Wicca, after Jack Gibb's Trust theory in humanist psychology.[191] "The

---

Embodied Mind and its Challenge to Western Thought (New York: Basic Books, 1999).
[190] Victor Turner *Ritual Process...* chapter 4, 131-165.
[191] Jack R. Gibb *Trust: A New View of Personal and Organizational*

kind of *communitas* desired… is a transformative experience that goes to the root of each person's being and finds in which root something profoundly communal and shared."[192]

Trust means not just trusting the fundamental goodwill of one's fellows but also trusting one's own ability, fundamental goodwill, right to be powerful and aware, desire to connect with the divine, and above all in the process of awakening and coming to power. Trust includes releasing all need to control the process or to control others or to attempt to control the spark of the Divine as it manifests in the Circle. Trust is an act of will, reinforced through experience.

Open-ness means opening to possibilities, opening to awareness, allowing oneself to become vulnerable and passive. By creating together a safe space in the ritual Circle and then opening up to whatever is there in oneself or in the divine purpose to do, paradoxically this conscious surrender to the divine creates greater and more effective exercise of the will as an effect - passive becomes powerful. Wiccans are always opening to power, to awaken and increase their ability together.

One cannot produce that perfect harmony that is desired, "perfect love and perfect trust"[193], simply by the mechanics of ritual. The open-ness and giving in to trust is an internal process facilitated by the influence of the divine, by the effectiveness of the blessings and magic working and by the theatrical pull of the ritual and it takes time to get over socially conditioned responses to

Development (Los Angeles: Guild of Tutors Press, 1978). Maphis 3rd and others *Pagans for Peace Tradition Book of Shadows* 1991-2008 mss in author's possession.
[192] Turner op cit, 138.
[193] This phrase is used to denote the ideal state of harmony in Wiccan groups.

things that might happen and to people in circle. Frequent practice of trance induction, as we shall see, is needed to achieve these goals.

Realization means coming to know the Higher Self - the part that is always most aware of the flow of the divine energies in the world, always most in tune, becoming aware of when one is centred and powerful and conscious.

Interdependence: Witches believe very much that it is good to be strong and capable and powerfully aware of who one is and what one can do. However, each one's strengths may cancel another's weaknesses and each will learn and grow together and become greater than either would be alone. Humans co-create one another in society and this value of being powerful with others strongly emphasizes the social components of personality.[194]

A Priest/ess is trained in visualization, symbolism, sacred movement and mudras, mythology and theatrical skills, concentration and meditation and a range of other skills and techniques, in particular techniques of magical ritual, that vary depending on the emphases of specific groups or teachers as s/he progresses up through the levels of trance experience and Priesthood training. The central experience and the axis around which all of the other training revolves is trace induction and the experiences derived from it and the incorporation of those experiences into the larger pattern of clergy work. Although this book refers to these other skills, they are seen as reinforcing and elaborating this central core in ecstatic trance, and not meaningful in themselves, secondary.

---

[194] This paragraph and the previous four were adapted from *Pagans for Peace Tradition Book of Shadows* 1991-2008 and based on Jack Gibb op cit.

There are eight specific magical techniques that Gerald Gardner and the first Wiccan covens used to a greater or lesser extent. Some are widely practiced now, others are not and practitioners have added ideas from elsewhere.[195] Wiccan clergy will undergo training in the use of each of these techniques. I will discuss most of them in detail in the next section.

1.   Meditation or Concentration
2.   Chants, spells, and invocations
3.   Projection of the astral body: There is a subtle energy body that surrounds the physical body, and is attached to it. It is said to contain the soul and the personal viewpoint. It is possible to enter a state of deep meditation and relaxation and imaginatively send the viewpoint self away from the physical body to explore either the physical world – to find out things at a distance or cause actions to happen or to explore the inner worlds or the non-physical realities often called the astral (star) realms.
4.   Trance, incense, drugs, wine
5.   Dancing
6.   Blood control, use of the cords
7.   The scourge[196]
8.   The Great Rite: The Great Rite is the central Mystery of Wicca as well as a technique for using and raising energy. It has already been discussed in depth.

Techniques of Trance Induction and Retrieval

Several of the eight magical techniques that Gerald Gardner talked about are also techniques for

---

[195] Janet and Stewart Farrar *Witches' Way,* 52.
[196] The scourge is a cat of nine tails, generally with tails made of braided embroidery thread – a symbolic whip.

inducing or deepening trance and in the interests of consistency I'll deal with them first. As well as techniques for inducing trance, a good Priestess or Priest must also know how to end a trance gently and how to bring a partner back to consensus reality and then to debrief them and assist them in incorporating whatever they learned or experienced back into their life. Wiccan clergy should undertake training in the use of each of the Gardnerian techniques at least, although physical limitations and taste mean that not everyone will practice all of them.

More important than any technique, first of all, are the qualities of character. The Priestess inducing trance must be trustworthy and disinterested – her purpose in inducing the trance must not be for her personal benefit. She must also be familiar with the various states of trance and an Initiate. The person undertaking the trance must be willing to surrender control in trust to the Priestess, trust the process and believe in her personal worthiness to experience the presence of the Goddess. Developing these qualities of character takes time – trust cannot be forced in the slightest.

The inducing Priestess must be sensitive to the flow of energy and able to push it and also to thoroughly ground herself and the recipient. She must be prepared for and able to ground an energetic backlash if the recipient is not quite ready to go deeper and also able to pour energy into her to drive her as far as her level of trust will take her.

There is a norm that a Wiccan Initiate must be a "proper person, properly prepared." Pragmatically, in addition to matters of knowledge this includes lifestyle issues and some values as well. To be blunt, unmedicated mental disorders cause harm to the individual who is not seeking help as well as their family

and friends and this should not be supported as a
legitimate lifestyle choice. Chronic unemployment and
underemployment causes harm as well, living in fantasy
rather than reality is unhealthy, and support for these
conditions does harm to the people living in them. All
clergy must complete faeces coagulation 101. They must
keep their personal lives generally in order. To begin
with they must have a regular and sufficient source of
income, a place to live and an adequate diet, no active
addictions, and reasonably stable lifestyle. This does not
mean that all clergy must live conventional mainstream
lifestyles. However, if a person cannot get their own life
in order they are manifestly not capable of helping others
to do so. Everyone experiences periods of upheaval but
someone in chronic crisis is not a "proper person,
properly prepared". The mere fact that some persons
choose in some way to harm themselves does not mean
that we are obliged to support their choices and to, in
fact, honour and celebrate their harm to themselves and
to others.

Those parts of the values or ideas of minority
communities that reinforce their outsider status are not
values that we can perpetuate and persons espousing
these values are not proper persons. Feminist politics
cannot be based on the rejection of heterosexuality as a
chosen option for women, nor can it be separatist and
anti-male, without condemning it to marginal
ineffectuality. Polyamoury must not include rejection of
a personal choice of monogamy nor the attempt to
undermine monogamy – the institution of compulsory
monogamy and the social and political frameworks that
do not give non-monogamous families the same
protection as monogamous ones are legitimate targets
for change. And so on. It is not that we reject the norm
outright, but that we wish to extend the norm and change
the values of society at large. Anything that smacks of
victim mentality or lack of respect for others should lead

one to question a person's preparation for Initiation or even clergy training.

Meditation or Concentration: this is fundamental and there are several well developed meditation techniques. Regular practice in meditation accustoms the practitioner to altered states of consciousness and teaches her to switch into and out of these states. This is for training the Will and is both a solo and group practice for Wiccans. Guided meditations and trance journeys, which are group practices, are ritual story telling sessions which take the participants to a place chosen by the ritual leader, often to meet the image of a Goddess or God or an elemental guardian spirit.

Meditation is a key technique in grounding – finding the core of oneself, connecting the life energy to the earth and keeping a sense of connection and belonging. In ritual, grounding is used to balance the energy of the practitioner and to dispose of unwanted or excess amounts of energy by pouring it into the Earth, which can absorb a huge amount of it. One grounds to become calm, to return to consensus reality after trance work, to draw energy from the Earth and connect back firmly to the body.

Chants, when repeated at great length, so that the often mundane lyrics blur completely and they become simply assortments of sound, work well. The gist of this kind of trance induction is focused boredom to create an altered state into which something else may come. This is not the same as the excellent energy-raising technique of the 'wordless chant' in which ritual participants simply open their throats and make sounds, which come to blend together into one large sound . Other techniques that rely on focused boredom are the long dance, or sortilege, or candle magick or other scrying techniques where the intention is to not simply enter a state of trance but to undertake a specific magickal action while there. This quality of chanting is why simple doggerel works better than complex and beautiful poetry in trance rituals.

Drugs, particularly hallucinogens but also soporifics and stimulants, are useful for shifting out of ordinary day-to-day reality and exploring other emotional and intuitive states, and asking for the Gods to come and play. They are very common in shamanic religions. Because one is more open when under the influence, energy not usually accessible can be called upon and used for magical purposes. Not all drugs have the same effects and so one must choose the one that suits the working - it is not useful to become drunk or incoherently stoned, and many drugs' effects are inconveniently long-lasting. As well, there are concerns about the legality of many drugs. A small amount of wine is relaxing and grounding at the end of a trance.

Dancing is an excellent way to enter a state of highly energized trance. The repetitive motion, repeated over a long period, usually very simple steps, causes the conscious mind to be both occupied and asleep so that the intuitive self can rise to the fore. Physical exertion raises the body's energy level and that tunes everything up to a higher pitch. Long-lasting slow dancing works to the end of focused boredom while more energetic, faster paced and complex dances like a spiral dance or snake dance (or even a long bout of square dancing or line dancing) eventually produces sensory overload and a 'floating' trance, another effective means of entering trance. The uncontrolled trances that people often experience at raves or other concerts and musical events are of this type – over-stimulation causing the critical part of the mind to shut down temporarily.

Blood control and the use of the cords- being tied up in a situation of trust is very calming and assists many people to slip into a meditative state. The method of tying restrains movement and the flow of blood but does not cause any pain or discomfort. The surrender in trust and the lack of stimulation, particularly if the person is blindfolded as well, are both keys to this technique. Under-stimulation is related to but not the same as the focused boredom technique.

The scourge: There are two ways of using the scourge for trance induction; with gentle rhythmic physical stimulation, on the one hand, and as a slightly more intense physical stimulation that raises the energy level in the body either through sexual excitement or the endorphin rush of very slight pain over a longer period of time.

These last two techniques are examples, as well, of a further general trance technique, similar to left-hand Tantra in India - pushing past taboos and discomfort to free oneself from unnecessary fears. Ritual nudity has a similar valuable effect on many people and by pushing past that boundary they release energy and become able to go deeper. The sexual symbolism and flavour of Wiccan ritual, particularly Drawing Down, with the kisses on the breasts and above the genitals and the touches on the naked body, are also taboo-breaking and thus release a great deal of power and encourage trance.

Magickal energy work can be used to push a person into trance (with their permission and under the right circumstances), and the expectations of a well-constructed ritual, with stages of trance built in, can walk a person right to the doorway. The capacity to move energy, both to push it out and to receive it, is essential to any magician, and both parties in DDM are magicians. Guided meditations or path-working rituals which tell a story and take people on an imaginative journey, either deep into the Earth or to some other realm altogether, are effective group trance techniques. They do not produce the intense experiences of some others but, because they are gradual and structured, they are easier paths to follow for early trance experiences. By using a story with mythological or symbolic value to the group, in the hands of a skilful story teller this trance can be combined with religious education as well.

So, the general techniques discussed so far are: focused boredom, rhythmic stimulation, guided meditation and trance journeys, drugs, sensory overload, sensory deprivation, left-hand boundary violation work. Any number of examples of these can be thought of, using different media – for example drumming can be slow and repetitive to be boring (but crucially a kind of boredom that requires that one continue to stay focused on the task regardless), or it can be fast and exciting and overwhelm the senses, it can be paired with dancing, or accent a guided meditation. Sex magick is an example of both boundary work and sensory overload.

To bring someone or a group of people back from trance. The first thing to do is to stop doing whatever was putting them under – stop drumming, stop pushing energy into them, stop dancing. Have a transition in the story of the trance journey to bring them back to consensus reality by walking back through the stages, back up through the rabbit hole or whatever. It is best to build a gentle transition into the script.

Then, if working one on one, ask the person to thank the Gods and spirits, remind them of their name and have them open their eyes. If they are having difficulty, wash their face, hands and feet with a cool wet cloth. Ask them what they remember from the journey, bless food and drink and share it (eating and drinking is very grounding). Be sure to ground afterward. Be sure to formally transition from the Circle back to the everyday world by thanking the Gods and the elements and taking down and releasing the astral temple created at the start of the Circle.

Once a person has achieved trance, it is much easier to get there again, and much easier to go deeper into it. With experienced and well-trained Priestesses and Priests the simplest trance induction statement is "Remember what it felt like the last time you were in trance." Technique is important only at the earliest stages although a strong set of associations can be built to make it easier to go further through a given technique. A trance, once achieved, can usually be made more intense and deeper by a process of repetition and suggestion.

The trance experience often leaves a 'halo' effect in which the person gradually returns to consensus reality. It is important to review the trance – to bring out whatever direct messages may have been delivered, to describe the sensations, emotions and more subtle feelings and impressions delivered. A brief debriefing and 'cooling off' period happens with sharing food and drink and the participants in the ritual will typically write an account of the experience in their magical journals.

Stages of Trance Ability and Experience

These principles can be illustrated by the concrete example of the experience of trance in the most common Wiccan trance induction ritual, *Drawing Down the Moon/Sun* and how it would be used in training in the apprehension of the mystical. *Drawing Down the Moon* is a ritual of ecstatic possession trance. Its purpose is to assist the Priestess to embody the spirit of the Goddess of the Wiccan religion, one of Whose most prominent symbols is the Moon. It is the principal ritual used in trance induction and is described in detail in earlier chapters. This ritual is valued for the theological reason that it is the means through which the Goddesses and Gods come into the Circle and directly interact with the members of the worship group. By possessing the bodies of the Priestess and Priest They directly are experienced, speak with, and can offer advice and help to the members of the coven.

In this discussion I will describe a typical Drawing Down in which the Priest induces trance in the Priestess and draws a Goddess into her, for convenience.

We can readily distinguish five stages of trance experience (that shade into one another – the boundaries are not as clear as this example and discussion might lead one to believe) and use the same ritual to induce each of them. 1. "Presence" trance, 2. "Oracular" trance, 3. "Prophetic" trance, 4. "Partial Possession" trance (with consciousness and volition), 5. "Full Possession".

In other words the Priestess goes from "I think I might have felt something" to full-blown possession trance in which she surrenders control of her body to a Goddess for a period of time (typically no more than several minutes although it can be longer). In large part it is a question of training and habituation. The idea of "perfect love and perfect trust" is absolutely essential – reaching the point of surrendering oneself in trust to the experience. The earlier discussion of the meaning-making process and the use of the TORI principles will be illustrated through this description. Training in the eight magical techniques discussed above will be concurrent with training in Drawing Down the Moon and will increase the ability to focus, enter and leave trance, and increase the level of comfort with functioning in an altered state of consciousness.

To summarize: after the circle is cast and the directions called, the Priest will bless the Priestess with the Five-fold Kiss, and then deliver an invocation of the Goddess while both projecting energy into the Priestess and pulling out from her. The Priestess will have grounded and surrendered in trust to the Priest. If she is experienced, she will likely be in a state of light trance before the end of the Five-fold Blessing. In some versions of Wicca, and in most cases when particular Goddesses or Gods are being called into the Circle, a series of short invocatory descriptions will be called out by the Priest as part of the ritual previously described. These may be scripted stock phrases or improvised and will be chosen to deepen the trance by adding texture to the experience – colours and clothing and attributes of particular deities will be described. Poetic names and allusions to myths will also be used.

The Priestess, now seen as embodying the Goddess, recites the *Charge of the Goddess*, a central theological statement of Wicca.[197] If she is in a deeper state of trance, she may choose (or the Goddess in her may so choose) to dispense with recitation in favour of prophetic statements, song, or dance – the recitation is seen as a fallback position should trance be light. The Priestess may then perform *Drawing Down the Sun* and call the God into the Priest, although that ritual is less common because Wicca is Goddess-primary. Some Wicca-identified neo-Pagan groups work only with Goddesses, but they are a minority.

From the repeated performance of this ritual, together with debriefing afterward and specific practice of skills in ritual and the eight types of Gardnerian magic, the several stages of trance are experienced.

---

[197] Janet and Stewart Farrar *Witches' Way* 297-8. This is the most common version of the Charge.

"Presence" trance- Wiccan theology is panentheistic and polytheistic. The Gods are seen as present and partly embodied in every aspect of the material world, as numerous individual beings with different sets of specific powers and interests. Human beings also differ and have different interests that predispose both humans and deities to form relationships with one another based on our affinities. So, a person who is strongly home and family oriented is more likely to have a relationship with the Goddess Vesta than with Artemis or Aphrodite, a kind and gentle person with Quan-yin rather than the Morrigan[198], and so on. So, while it is possible to initially draw a generic energy of the divine female or divine male into a person, in general that kind of identification is only useful in this earliest stage of trance induction and is often replaced by the invocation or evocation of specific deities as training progresses.

Although all Gods of both sexes and a range of genders are available for Drawing Down, at the earliest stages usually only the most generic (the female principle and the male principle) and the sex that corresponds to the physical sex of the person having the deity Drawn into them are invoked. The Gods may have Their own opinions and quite frequently a specific Goddess or God will come into the person and claim them as Their servant. This is a highly prized development and is one goal of the initial stages of mystical training – to acquire a Matron (and potentially also a Patron) deity to oversee and participate in the Wiccan's training. In a polytheistic religion people have

[198] Vesta – Roman Goddess of the sacred hearth fire, corresponding to Greek Hestia. Artemis - Green Goddess of the woods and independent female power as well as midwifery. Aphrodite – Greek Goddess of sexuality and female beauty. Quan-yin – Chinese Goddess/boddhisvata of compassion and kindness. The Morrigan – Irish triple Goddess of warfare and destructive female power. These Goddesses are listed for illustrative purposes – Wiccans can, and do, call upon Goddesses and Gods from many times and places.

relationships of respect and worship with a number of different Goddesses and Gods. Generally, however, Wiccans are really close and tight with only a couple of deities and have friendly but more distant relationships with the others.

There are generally three ways that Matron or Patron relationships are formed (and, by the way, these relationships are not always exclusive, although they usually are, and people may have these relationships with different deities as they change and grow):

1) The God chooses. For whatever reason, or for no reason that anyone can tell a Goddess or God will tap a person on the shoulder and say, "you are mine." Sometimes it's as clear as that, but more often the realization of Her or His interest grows – one may find images of black cats and actual black cats coming to be more common in their life, in odd coincidental moments, or a particular word or name of a deity will keep appearing in reading material, or dreams will prompt investigation until the realization dawns that Bast wants to have him as Her servant.

2) As a person comes to a clearer understanding of who they fundamentally are and sees that a particular Goddess or God represents the best and strongest expression of the type of person – an animal lover who strikes up a relationship with Pan as the shepherd and "Piper at the Gates of Dawn," protector of the animals, or a hunter who connects with Herne the hunter and hunted, a homebody who connects with Hestia and so on.

3) The Goddess or God represents or embodies something that they desire to be and She or He will help them to become stronger in that area of life. For example a person who wanted to be more eloquent would work with Mercury, a person who wanted to be more graceful

and attractive would connect with Freda Erzulie, and someone who wanted to hone their skills would get together with Lugh or Brigid.

In all cases, this is not something for nothing. The Gods demand that a person do the work and that serve them wholeheartedly in their areas of particular interest, in return for Their help. This points us back to the problem of ethical behaviour –making agreements with the Gods obliges one to uphold their end of the agreement. Be careful what you agree to and be careful that you know Whom you are serving – a War Goddess like the Morrigan is not a kindly Mother and She dislikes being treated like one, The God Dionysus does not like people who are inclined to temperate behaviour but demands passionate excess, and so on.

It's rather like having a powerful friend who takes one on as a protégé. In the great old Roman tradition, a powerful person was evaluated by the number and quality of their protégés and in more recent times there are "Old Boy's networks" of graduates of elite schools who advance the interests of deserving young talent from their school. In other words, devoting yourself to the God does not automatically guarantee you Their wholehearted support – it has to be earned – but that devotion gets Their attention.

So, after the first performance of the ritual of Drawing Down the Moon, the student will be asked by her/his teacher; "did you feel anything, and what was it like?" Typically a student will have felt a mild physical sensation of some sort – a tingling, or a sense of presence, without a name or a face. Further questions will pull out details and allow the student to build a stronger memory around that initial sensation. Often DDM will immediately be repeated, so that the student can use the new memory as a key to move closer toward the ultimate goal of possession trance. New details may emerge at this point, to be added to the picture. Wiccan theology recognizes that the picture drawn of the deity is an imaginative doorway into a realm of experience rather than necessarily being a factual description of Who really connected with the person having the experience. Beliefs are tools and the imaginative elaboration and intensification of beliefs and experiences is a valuable skill to learn. Learning and practicing this skill is a conscious goal of the training process for Wiccan teachers.[199]

The "Presence" trance stage may last for several months, although it will deepen and become more intense each time Drawing Down is done. Practice will cause habituation and increased comfort with the trance state. At some point the sense of presence will resolve into the presence of a particular individual deity, Who may or may not tell the student Her/His name. The student will be encouraged to ask and to continue to imaginatively build as clear a picture of the physical attributes and presence of the deity as possible.

"Oracular " trance - the student will have been instructed to write down what was learned during the DDM experience and to go home and cast a circle and ask for guidance at least once, and preferably several times, before the next time the student and instructor got together. She will be reinforcing the experience and asking that it be a doorway through that the Goddess or God will speak with her and guide her progress. This reinforcement and personal spiritual practice will continue to be required throughout a Wiccan's training, and into their life, to keep the insights fresh and alive. Wiccans are expected to keep journals recording their ritual and trance experiences for reference.

---

[199] T. M. Luhrmann *Persuasions*. Luhrmann's discussion of the acculturation of modern Britons into ritual magic bears on this point, in particular her chapter 21 on "interpretive drift", pages 307-323.

With Oracular trance the deity will speak through the student. S/he will offer advice or deliver an observation or a comment. Words and often other sensations, sometimes movements and gestures, sometimes images or smells or whole songs, will come to the student. This is a breakthrough stage that must be celebrated, and typically marks the point of First Degree Initiation– the God will use this door and progress now will be more rapid. The details of the oracle should be preserved and reflected on since they will bear on the future direction of the student or whomever she was directed to speak it to.

The Oracular stage marks the beginning of a Priestess' independent creation of ritual: now she is expected to be able to receive material directly from the Gods to include in her ritual composition.

The stage of "prophetic" trance is closely linked to this one. Whereas the oracle broke through, because of further practice the student is now able to induce trance reliably and start to consciously go deeper. She has established a relationship with her Matron/Patron and is developing it both consciously through study and involvement in ritual centred on her deities but also through a stronger openness to them and to being personally changed by them – to move more like they might move, talk like them, and intensify the way that her being in the world reflects their style. Ginette Paris' books are very helpful descriptions of this process of identification with one's Matron, although from a Jungian, not Wiccan, perspective.[200]

"Partial Possession" happens when the Goddess takes over the body of the Priestess, with her consent, while the Priestess remains conscious and aware. In general the first time this happens it is only for a few

---

[200] Ginette Paris *Pagan Meditation* and *Pagan Grace* op cit.

seconds – a highly intensified state of presence trance or oracular trance is followed by a brief interval in which the Goddess is moving the body, seeing through the eyes, speaking. Even with considerable preparation and complete consent, it is so terrifying to give up control of the body that this first experience can only be sustained for seconds. It often becomes a merger with the person as the principal force in the body but informed by the continued presence of the God, to collapse back to consensus reality after a few minutes. Typically this is the point of Second Degree Initiation, as the Initiation is intended to open the door more widely and add extra energy into the mix.

Those who are with the person during the interval of partial possession will note changes in the physical appearance, posture, enunciation, and movement of the person. They will also be expected to feel a sense of power, experience awe and perhaps heat or cold or some physical sensations themselves.

"Full Possession" happens only rarely to even highly experienced Witches, due to the difficulty of surrendering ego control for more than a brief interval. It is the stage where the body is inhabited by the conscious divine and the person is an observer only, and may not be aware of what happened except in brief snatches throughout. It lasts for several minutes to hours and is very hard on the body. The deity will act as it wishes and with the full consent of its host to perform ritual or healing and to transform the host. At this stage the Third Degree Initiation occurs and the Great Rite is possible. The Great Rite is a hieros gamos, discussed in depth and detail elsewhere, and is the central symbol of the Wiccan relationship to the divine.[201]

---

[201] Samuel Wagar "The Wiccan Great Rite: hieros gamos in the Modern West" in *Journal of Religion and Popular Culture*, summer 2009

Although the Great Rite is highly valued, requiring its performance for Third Degree Initiation borders on sexual coercion, that is seen as blasphemous as well as evil. As sex is sacred and the bodies of women and men are holy, any non-consensual sexual activity is blasphemous. However, there is an expectation that all Third Degrees will practice the Great Rite, where appropriate partners are available, because of its central importance. The Great Rite is the preferred option for Third Degree Initiation, when possible.

In some Wiccan Traditions (denominations), including Pagans for Peace Tradition (in which I am a 3rd degree High Priest) , in order to receive the Third Degree a person must be capable of full possession trance involving both Goddesses and Gods, regardless of their personal sex or gender. This emphasizes the transcendent quality of the divine and the arbitrariness of gender and sexual division and points toward the realization of the divine androgyne in the individual.

From the first attempt to do Drawing Down the Moon to Third Degree typically takes five to six years of practice. A rare Talented person with a great deal of will and application can manage it in three years. Drawing Down and trance work are not the only training or knowledge required of Wiccan clergy, although these things are seen as central, informing the other aspects of training, and essential to the spiritual growth and authority of Priestesses and Priests. A person who has not experienced the transformative mysteries and been Initiated is not considered qualified as a religious leader by British Traditional Wiccans.

The relationship between the Inner Court Mysteries described above and the Outer Court public or semi-public rituals is complex. Outer Court ritual and symbolism is not just for show. As Victor Turner put it, in his discussion of *communitas*; the state of spontaneous *communitas* and ecstatic trance is a means to the end of becoming more fully involved in the role-playing of life in general.[202] This power must be transformed to be applied to the organizational details of social existence and ecstasy cannot substitute for lucid thought and sustained will. However, social-structural action becomes arid and mechanical where those involved in it are not periodically immersed in *communitas*, with its temporary erasure of distinctions and ecstatic affirmation of our common human and animal natures.[203] "Spontaneous *communitas* is nature in dialogue with structure...together they make up one stream of life."[204]

Although Wiccan Outer Court rituals don't directly tell or show the Mystery or the details of rituals used in Inner Court to produce trance, the symbolism must allude to the Mystery and the ritual must be so informed by that energy that it contains and raises real power for participants, power that resembles that of the Mystery and acts as preparation for that work for those not yet "proper people, properly prepared," and a reminder to those who are. Often this is ensured by a private preliminary to the ritual in which Drawing Down is performed on the ritual leaders so that they enact the ritual as personifications of the Goddess and God, in a 'halo' of light trance.

Versions of the Drawing Down ritual, symbolic reinterpretations of the Great Rite and some quotations of key phrases taken directly from the Drawing Down ritual will often be included in the Outer Court rituals as well. They have the same ritual structure, with the quartered circle, the invocations of the Watchtowers and the calling of elemental guardians[205]. Inner Court is more

---

[202] Turner, op cit 139.
[203] Turner op cit, 139.
[204] Turner op cit, 140.
[205] Symbolic figures asked to guard each of the directions around the ritual space and to admit specific kids of spiritual energy into it.

focused and direct, partly due to practice and familiarity both with the material and the people involved (in a closed, small group, with few guests) and with a smaller number of people with differing expectations to satisfy.

Inner Court and Outer Court differ in a number of details – Inner Court frequently works nude, involves magick working, trance induction and oracular trance, divination, pathworking and Drawing Down the Moon and Sun. Outer Court is more likely to involve ritual theatre, the use of robes, dancing and movement, guided meditations, spiral or long dance and energy raising (including group trance induction through dance) and grounding. Chanting, singing, and music are more prominent features of Outer Court rituals.

There are particular skills that have to be taught for effective Outer Court, Priestly Ministry, in addition to the skills of a coven Priestess.

The clergy and the various Temples that they serve are aware of the difficult juggling involved – bringing forward the insights derived from the intensely individual and personal experience of trance and revelation to be useful to people that have not experienced it, deriving social insights and values from personal experiences, fitting these Imagistic visions into the quotidian realities of rules of behaviour and ethical statements that people can use to live their lives as non-mystics. It cannot just be for show or it is a sham, lying to the clergy and congregants about the true and sacred core of the religion in the Mysteries. But at the same time, rituals cannot be interpreted literally, the symbolism must not simply reinforce the state of things as they already are but must point toward the transformative Mysteries and their value in human life without stating them directly.

The danger, as may have happened with Christianity[206], is that the public Outer Court will come to be seen as the real thing and the only version of Wicca unless Wiccan clergy continue to practice the Mysteries and constantly refer back to them in other work. The Inner Court can be informed, in turn, by the Outer, can reflect back some of the concerns and issues of even the much broader society, in an intertextual dance of reference, self-reference and modification. The Gods do not only speak to the broadest ethical concerns but frequently offer practical advice. But the Source has to be in the mystical, Mysteries, experience or the religion simply becomes of the society rather than of the spirit, mundane and quotidian rather than meaning-making, reflecting rather than refracting. When religion becomes too much of the world it loses its capacity to comment on the world and even the necessity to challenge the categories of the world. That transcendent element is vital to become deeper and greater than this.

Religion, to survive, cannot be simply a social club with a values centre, but must be a force for personal and social critique and transformation. And ritual cannot simply be values-informed theatre. Both must reach deeper into the person and facilitate change and spiritual connection and growth. But religious bodies satisfy a range of social needs – for friendships, for cruising and dating, for art and theatre, for business and personal networking, for identity and belonging.

For a religion to persist past the first generation as well it must find ways, both Imagistic and Doctrinal, to pass along its insights about human nature, the good life, and the Gods, to the children and new converts.

---

[206] Timothy Freke and Peter Gandy *The Jesus Mysteries* (London: Thorsons, 1999) and Barrie Wilson *How Jesus Became Christian* (Toronto: Random House, 2008) both deal with the relationship between the Mysteries traditions and the Christ movement in the first couple of centuries c.e.

Periodic community celebrations and religious retreats have become an important part of the process for many Wicca-identified Pagans although camp-out weekends in the summer and "eight parties a year" (where children are often not welcome) cannot ensure the necessary retention of the younger generation and the passing on of the lore. The establishment of Outer Court Temple groups is a move toward this necessary religious growth.

As the Wiccan religion continues to grow, and as the Outer Court Temple groups continue to grow, these issues become more pressing. The great majority of Wicca-identified Pagans are not Initiates, and will never be Initiates. A substantial fraction of the people practicing in informal groups is also not qualified by the standards of the conservative British Traditions and the democratic tone of anti-intellectualism and anti-elitism eats away at the legitimacy of this more challenging path. The synergy between Imagistic and Doctrinal is a key to keeping both alive and healthy – the flash of the spirit and intense experience for the few and the structure that brings those insights down to Earth for the day-to-day inspiration of the many - and the development of linked Inner and Outer Court groups is a positive development for the religion, still working itself out in practice.

Appendix A : Contemporary standard ritual script

Hecate-Legba Coven
Standard ritual format
November 5th '99

The usual set up with a small altar at each quarter and a larger one, holding food and drink, at the north. Tools plus whatever materials are needed for performing rituals are set at the appropriate direction.

The Circle is swept and cast as follows:
The Priestess sweeps the area with a broom counterclockwise.

She then casts the circle with the sword, saying "This is a Place that is not a Place and a Time that is not a Time", while circling around 3 times clockwise. She leaves a doorway.

The other members of the coven are pulled one by one into the circle, which is then closed off.

The five directions are called:

EAST/AIR:Guardians of the Watchtower of the East,
Come and Guard our Circle
Let through the power of air
Clear thinking, freshness, possibility,
Blessed Be

SOUTH/FIRE:Guardians of the Watchtower of the South
Come and Guard our Circle
Let through the power of fire
to bring us courage to face and overcome our fears

Blessed Be

WEST/WATER:Guardians of the Watchtower of the West
Come and Guard our Circle
Let through the power of water
to connect us to one another, the power of love and caring.
Blessed Be.

NORTH/EARTH:Guardians of the Watchtower of the
North
Come and Guard our Circle
Let through the power of earth -
Flags, flax, frig and fodder , the good things of this life.
Blessed Be.

CENTRE/SPIRIT:Guardians of above and below
Come and Guard our Circle
Let through the power of the spirit
to open our eyes and our hearts,
to move us to act rightly in the world
Blessed BE.

and then the following (the Charge of the Goddess) is
recited:

Whenever you have need of anything
once in the month, and best when the moon is full
assemble in some secret place
and adore the spirit of me, who is queen of all Witches.

There assemble, you who wish to learn all sorcery
but have not yet won its deepest secrets.
To these will I teach the mysteries.

And you shall be free from slavery
and as a sign that you are truly free
you shall be naked in your rites;
and you shall dance and sing and feast,
make music and love, all in my praise.

I who am the beauty of the green Earth
and the white Moon among the stars
and the mystery of the waters
and the desire of the heart,
I call unto your soul.

Arise and come unto me.

For I am the soul of nature
who gives life to the Universe.
From me all things proceed
and unto me all things return.

Let my worship be within the heart that rejoices
For behold, all acts of love and pleasure are my rituals.

And therefore, let there be beauty and strength,
power and compassion, honour and humility
mirth and reverence within you.

And you who seeks for me
know that your seeking and yearning
will fail unless you know the mystery -
if that which you seek you do not find within you,
then you wil never find it outside.

Behold, I have been with you since the beginning
and I am that which is attained at the end of desire.

{ **Drawing Down the Moon**

This is the ritual of incarnation through which the Goddess
is invited to take over the body of Her Priestess.

In recognition of the special divinity in the Priestess give
her the Five-fold kiss to begin (kiss each of the named
parts):}

Blessed be thy feet, which have led thee in these ways.
Blessed be thy womb, without which we would not be.
Blessed be thy hands, which reach out and act in the
world.
Blessed be thy breasts, formed in beauty and strength.
Blessed be thy lips, which speak the sacred names.
Blessed be you,
Priestess and Witch,
Daughter of the Goddess.

{ Make the 1st degree symbol (right nipple, left nipple,
pubic hair, right nipple) as you say:}

I invoke thee and call upon thee, Mighty Mother of us all,
Bringer of all fruitfulness:
By seed and root, by stem and bud, by leaf and flower and
fruit do I invoke thee to descend upon the body of this, thy
servant and Priestess.

Hail Aradia! From the Amalthean horn pour forth thy store
of love.

I lowly bend before thee, I adore thee to the end,
with loving sacrefice thy shrine adorn.
Thy foot is to my lip, my prayer upborn upon the rising
insense smoke.

Then spend thine ancient love, Oh Mighty One, descend to
aid me, who without thee am forlorn.

ARADIA, who calls us to rise up against oppression,
Queen of the Witches, daughter of Diana, Stormqueen,
Crow, Raven.

ARTEMIS, Bear Goddess, huntress, woman of the
wildlands, untamed power, sister to all women, midwife.

ASTARTE, Queen of Heaven, Fiery Star, Sacred Tree at the centre of the universe, Olive.

NIMUE, Merlin's successor, Initiator, Magician, Lady of the Lake who recognizes the True King.

DANA, Mother of the waters, flowing rivers of the land and spirit, guardian of dreams and visions, defender of boundaries.

ISIS, Celestial Cow, whose milk is the Nile, All-Mother, First and Greatest Goddess.

STAR GODDESS, whose arms encircle the universe, whose body is the dark of night and the glowing stars.

Descend upon the body of this, your Priestess.

I invoke thee and call upon thee, Mighty Mother of us All, Bringer of all Fruitfulness.

By seed and root, by stem and bud, by leaf and flower and fruit do I invoke thee to descend upon the body of this thy servant and Priestess.

{ **Drawing Down The Sun**

After the Priestess has recovered from the shock of DDM, she does Drawing Down the Sun and invites the God to take over the body of the Priest.

She gives him the Five-fold kiss, as follows:}

Blessed be thy feet, which have led thee in these ways.
Blessed be thy sex, without which we would not be.
Blessed be thy hands, which reach out and act in the world.
Blessed be thy breast, formed in beauty and strength.

Blessed be thy lips, which shall speak the sacred names.
Blessed be you,
Priest and Witch,
Son of the God.

{The Priestess steps back a pace and kneels and she says:}

Deep calls on height, the Goddess on the God,
On Him who is the flame that quickens her;
Let the hammer strike the anvil,
Let the lightening strike the Earth,
Let the Lance ensoul the Grail,
Let magic come to birth.

{ She touches with her right forefinger his throat, left hip,
right breast, left breast, right hip, and throat again. She
then spreads her hands outward, palms forward and
continues to invoke:}

In Her Name do I invoke Thee
Mighty Father of us all,

Lugh the tool-maker with your skillful hands

Pan the All-Father, All-Devourer, Piper at the Gates of
Dawn

Papa Legba , Guardian of the Thresholds, who stands at
the portal between the worlds

Hades, God of Death, Who tends the dead and prepares
them for rebirth, Dark One

Cernunnos, the Horned One, Lord of the Animals and the
Great Hunt, Lover of the Goddess

Raven, Trickster, Who creates and destroys with one
breath, goblin god, chaos

Green God, Grain God who dies that we may eat, lustful life, death that serves life

Come in answer to my call!
Descend, I pray thee, in thy servant and Priest.

{ She stands and takes a step back, the Priest makes the sign of fire toward her and says:}

I am the flame that burns in the heart of every man
And in the core of every star.
I am life and the giver of life, yet therefore is the knowledge of me
also the knowledge of death.

Let there be light.

{After DDM/S the main body of the coven meeting commences.}

{ Our standard food and drink blessing is as follows - spoken while holding up the wine goblet full of wine and the plate full of cakes - by any member of the coven :}

"It is not I who bless food and drink
but they who bless us,
for in their nature they nourish our bodies
and in the sharing of food and drink we create community."

A period of fellowship will be followed by dismissing the directions in reverse order:

Thank You Goddess
Thank You God

Spirit - Thank You for blessing us with increased understanding.
North - Thank you for making this our home.
West - Thank you for our connection and caring.
South - Thank you for the courage needed to do the work in our lives.
East - We end as we begin, with the breath of life.

The Circle is Open But Unbroken.
Merry Meet and Merry Part and Merry Meet Again.

Some Definitions

Different Traditions of Wicca have some differences around these definitions, but not great big ones, but I am going to go with Pagans for Peace Tradition's list, because that's where I am coming from, and mention some others in passing.

INNER COURT - The coven, consisting, usually, only of Initiated Wiccan clergy. Guests are rare, by invitation only. Typically performs more challenging and advanced work with a higher amount of trust required. The expectations on members are larger as well.

OUTER COURT - The group of students and friends of the coven. Membership by invitation and at the discretion of Priestess and Priest of coven. Performs celebratory work, seasonal observations and classes in various Pagan and Wiccan topics.

TRADITION - a "denomination" in Wicca - typically a group of covens and their Outer Court groups which practice following a similar set of rituals and whose Priestesses and Priests descend through a line of Initiation from a common source.

WICCA - A Pagan religion. There are a number of definitions of this word and a fair amount of argument - ranging from "anyone, pretty well regardless of what they believe or practice, who wants to call themselves Wiccan, is" to "Wicca is an Initiatory Mystery religion of clergy, practiced in small private groups whose rituals are secret to the uninitiated." Pagans for Peace Tradition accepts the second definition. Our Outer Court groups are practicing Wicca-influenced Paganism, and our public activities are also, but only the coven Inner Court work is Wicca.

MYSTERY - A Mystery is an ultimate fact of life which can only be experienced and which continues to grow in depth and complexity as we live. It is impossible to exhaust the meanings of Love, or Death, or Sex, or any other Mystery in a single lifetime. A Mystery is not a secret. To say that Wicca is a Mystery religion is to say that we have mystical experience at the centre, techniques to lead to experiencing these ultimate facts directly (or as much as possible).

TRANCE - an altered state of consciousness, similar to a hypnotic state, in which a person is more open to experience, with the critical and logical facilities reduced. Practice is needed to get good at switching this state on and coming back from it, and a high degree of trust helps. It is necessary for the exploration of the Mysteries, particularly for Drawing Down.

DRAWING DOWN THE MOON / SUN - DDM/S is a ritual of possession trance through which the Priestess and Priest invite the Goddess (in general as the feminine principle or a specific Goddess) and the Horned God (ditto) to come into their bodies. Typically the Goddesses are asked to come into the body of the Priestesses and the Gods into the Priest, but Pagans for Peace Tradition requires all 3rd degrees too be able to embody both Goddesses and Gods. There are several stages through which the experience passes (and generally it takes some tome of practice to get to the highest states of trance, and some people rarely or never get there). In brief - 1. a sense of "presence", 2. a deity delivers a message then leaves, 3. a deity hangs around but the Priestess maintains control 4. the deity moves the body, speaks or sings or whatever, 5. full possession trance (generally lasts for only a few minutes to an hour)

SKYCLAD - Ritual nudity is practiced in British Traditional Wiccan groups as the usual coven practice. If you attend Pagan religious retreats there will be nude swimming and casual nudity as well. Nudity has several valuable symbolic meanings: 1. it symbolizes innocence, trust and openness, 2. it recognizes the central importance of the body as the vehicle for spirit, 3. it symbolizes the equality of all ritual participants, 4. it is light-hearted and playful, 5. it pushes people past their usual boundaries. It is a Mystery. It is erotic but not explicitly sexual - because the only times the great majority of people get naked with other people is during sex, we have that association but that's very much not all that there is.

INITIATION - Initiation literally means to start something. There are doors in the spirit that lead to different stages of development and understanding. Generally speaking, people have to be shown the doorways and there are specific training processes and rituals to prepare them to find them and open the doors. British Trad Wicca has three stages of Initiation (a fourth, "dedicant" is sometimes added to signify that a person is a serious student in the Outer Court group) - they have different names so are usually referred to by number: 1st degree is a student level and the level at which a person becomes a coven member - they have some knowledge and skill but are very much still sponges doing it for themselves; 2nd degree has had some mystical experiences of trance and direct connection with the Gods and they are teaching some others, plus they can lead a coven in worship pretty well with a partner, write rituals, go into trance and out again; 3rd degree is a fully independent Priestess or Priest, with a wide ranging knowledge base, experience and ability in many areas, theologically innovative. 1st is for oneself, 2nd is for the coven or group, 3rd is for the Gods and the broader community.

POLYTHEISM, ATHEISM / AGNOSTICISM, PANTHEISM, PANENTHEISM, DUOTHEISM, MONOTHEISM - People that call themselves Wiccan approach the question of the divine in a variety of ways, ranging from a belief that the Gods are purely symbols for features of the natural world or of human life and experience to a literal belief in many individual Goddesses and Gods. The most usual way that you'll see Wicca-identified people talking are about the Great Goddess and Her Consort the Horned God of the animals (in which all Goddesses are said to be aspects of one Goddess, all Gods of one God - this DUOTHEISM is often reduced to a version of MONOTHEISM because the two are said to also be aspects of one great creative and destructive force). Often Wiccans are practical POLYTHEISTS, working with many faces of the divine, seen as separate individual Goddesses and Gods with Whom we can interact. Although Wiccans do not separate the divine from the world, seeing whatever version of divinity that we interact with as truly present here and now in the world of nature, we differ on whether the Gods are completely inside the world (PANTHEISM - all is Goddess, or ANIMISM -all things have their own special spirit) or partly inside and partly outside the world (PANENTHEISM).

In Pagans for Peace Tradition we are POLYTHEIST, PANENTHEIST and we use DUOTHEIST symbols when we speak of the feminine or masculine aspects of the Gods in general terms. Our focus is on religious experience, through trance, which gives us a direct experience of the presence of the Gods, and the theology which derives from that.

Bibliography

Adler, Margot, *Drawing Down the Moon: Witches, Druids, Goddess-Worshippers and other Pagans in America Today* (Boston: Beacon Press, 1979)

Anderson, Benedict *Imagined Communities: Reflections on the Origin and Spread of Nationalism* (London: Verso, 1983)

Asbell, Bernard, *The Pill: A Biography of the Drug that Changed the World*, (New York: Random House, 1995)

Ashcroft, Bill, Gareth Griffiths and Helen Tiffin *Post-Colonial Studies: The Key Concepts* (London: Routledge, 2000)

Atwood, Margaret *The Penelopiad* (Toronto: Alfred Knopf Canada, 2005)

Bell, Catherine *Ritual Theory, Ritual Practice,* (New York: Oxford University Press, 1992)
_____ *Ritual; Perspectives and Dimensions* (New York: Oxford U Press, 1997).
_____ ed., *Teaching Ritual* (New York: Oxford U Press, 2007).

Berger, Helen A., Evan A. Leach and Leigh S. Shaffer. *Voices from the Pagan Census: A National Survey of Witches and neo-Pagans in the United States.* Columbia SC: University of South Carolina Press, 2003.

Homi K. Bhabha *The Location of Culture* (London: Routledge, 1994),

Bibby, Reginald *Fragmented Gods – the poverty and potential of religion in Canada* 1987 Toronto: Stoddart, 1990
_____ *Unknown Gods: the ongoing story of religion in Canada* Toronto: Stoddart, 1993

_____ *Restless Gods – the renaissance of religion in Canada* Toronto: Stoddart, 2002

_____ *Restless Churches – how Canada's churches can contribute to the emerging religious renaissance* Kelowna BC: Wood Lake Books, 2004

_____ *The Boomer Factor – What Canada's Most Famous Generation is leaving behind* Toronto: Bastian Books, 2006

Bible, The Holy New American Standard Version.

Bourdieu, Pierre *Outline of a Theory of Practice* translated Richard Nice (1972, Cambridge: Cambridge U Press, 1977).

Bowker, John ed, *The Oxford Dictionary of Wqorld Religions* (Oxford: Oxford University Press, 1997)

Braude, Ann, *Radical Spirits: Spiritualism and Women's Rights in Nineteenth-Century America* (Boston: Beacon Press, 1989).

Brown, Callum G. *The Death of Christian Britain.* London: Routledge, 2001.

Z. Budapest *The Feminist Book of Lights and Shadows* (Venice CA: Luna Publications, 1976). (revised and reprinted as *The Holy Book of Women's Mysteries* (Oakland: Susan B. Anthony Coven, 1979)

Calasso, Roberto *The Marriage of Cadmus and Harmony*, translated by Tim Parks, (NY:Knopf, 1993)

Califia, Pat and Drew Campbell eds *Bitch Goddess: The Spiritual Path of the Dominant Woman* (San Francisco CA: Greenery Press, 1997)

Carnes, Mark C. *Secret Ritual and Manhood in Victorian America* (New Haven CT; Yale U Press, 1989).

Chakrabarty, Dipesh. *Provincializing Europe: Postcolonial Thought and Historical Difference.* Princeton: Princeton University Press, 2000.

Crowley, Aliester. *The Book of the Law*. 1904, reprint York
        Beach ME: Samuel Weiser,1976.
        _____. *Magick in Theory and Practice*. 1929, reprint New
        York: Dover, 1976.

Dahr, Janet, *Wild Women Witches of Greater Vancouver:
        Gyn/Ecology*, an unpublished M.A. thesis in the
        Department of Women Studies, Simon Fraser
        University, 1995.

Davis, Wade *Passage of Darkness: The Ethnobiology of the
        Haitian Zombie*, (Chapel Hill NC: University of
        North Carolina Press, 1988)

Maya Deren *Divine Horsemen: The Living Gods of Haiti*
        (1953, reprinted Kingston NY: MacPherson and
        Company, 1988),

Deveney, John Patrick *Paschal Beverly Randolph*, (Albany:
        State University of New York Press, 1997).

Dixon, Joy. *Divine Feminine: Theosophy and Feminism in
        England*. Baltimore: John Hopkins University Press,
        2001.

Eliade, Mircea *The Myth of the Eternal Return*, translated
        Willard R. Trask, (1954, revised edition Princeton:
        Princeton University Press 1971)

Eliot, T.S. *Murder in the Cathedral* (1935, London: Faber and
        Faber, 1965)., 23.

Farrar, Janet and Stewart Farrar. *Eight Sabbats for Witches*
        (London: Robert Hale, 1981)
        _____*The Witches Way: Principles, Rituals and Beliefs of
        Modern Witchcraft*. London: Robert Hale 1984.

Fields, Rick *How the Swans Came to the Lake – A narrative
        history of Buddhism in America* 1981, Boston MA:
        Shambhala, 1992

Foucault, Michel. *The History of Sexuality, Volume 1, An Introduction,* translated by Robert Hurley (1976, 1978 New York: Vintage Books / Random House, 1990)

_____. "Of Other Spaces" trans. Jay Miskowiec *Diacritics* 16.1 (Spring, 1986), 22-27.

_____, *The Archaeology of Knowledge and The Discourse on Language* translated by A. M. Sheridan Smith (1971, New York Pantheon/Random House, 1972)

Frankfurt, Harry G. *On Bullshit* (Princeton: Princeton University Press, 2004).

Freeman, Jo *The Tyranny of Structurelessness* (1970, reprinted Montreal: Bevy of Anarchist Feminists, 1986)

Freke, Timothy and Peter Gandy *The Jesus Mysteries* (London: Thorsons, 1999)

Gardner, Gerald B. *Keris and Other Malay Weapons*, B. Lumsden Milne ed. (Singapore: Progressive Publishing Company, 1936).

_____ *Witchcraft Today.* London; Robert Hale 1954, reprint New York: Magickal Childe, 1982.

Gibb, Jack R *Trust: A New View of Personal and Organizational Development* (Los Angeles: Guild of Tutors Press, 1978).

Gladwell, Malcolm *The Tipping Point; how little things can make a big difference*, New York; Back Bay / Little, Brown, 2000, 2002.

Godwin, Joscelyn *The Theosophical Enlightenment* (Albany: State University of New York Press, 1994).

Greer, John Michael *Inside A Magical Lodge: Group Ritual in the Western Tradition* (St. Paul: Llewellyn, 1998).

Greenwood, Susan Magic, Witchcraft and the Otherworld,; An Anthropology (Oxford: Berg, 2000).

Heselton, Philip, *Wiccan Roots: Gerald Gardner and the Modern Witchcraft Revival,* (Chielveley , UK: Capall Bann Publishing, 2000)

Hillman, James *A Terrible Love of War* (New York: Penguin Press, 2004)

Hirsch, Alan *The Forgotten Ways; reactivating the missional church* Grand Rapids MI, Brazos Press, 2006.

Howe, Ellic, *The Magicians of the Golden Dawn: A Documentary History of a Magical Order 1887-1923* (London: Routledge and Kegan Paul, 1972)

Hutton, Ronald. *The Triumph of the Moon: a History of Modern Pagan Witchcraft.* Oxford: Oxford University Press, 1999.

Johnson, Olive Skene *The Sexual Spectrum: Why We're All Different* (Vancouver: Raincoast, 2007).

James, William, *The Varieties of Religious Experience* (1902, republished New York: Barnes and Noble Books, 2004)

Kaldera, Raven ed. *Dark Moon Rising: Pagan BDSM and the Ordeal Path* (Hubbardston MA: Asphodel Press, 2006).
_____*Pagan Polyamory; Becoming a Tribe of Hearts* (Woodbury MN; Llewellyn Worldwide, 2005).

Kelly, Aidan. *Crafting the Art of Magic Book 1: A History of Modern Witchcraft. 1939-1964* .St. Paul MN: Llewellyn Publications, 1991 (revised and republished as *Inventing Witchcraft: A Case Study in the Creation of a New Religion* (Loughborough UK: Thoth Publications 2007))

Kippenberg, Hans G. *Discovering Religious History in the Modern Age* translated Barbara Harshaw (Princeton: Princeton U Press, 2002).

Korzybski, Alfred *Science and Sanity: An Introduction to Non-Aristotelian Systems and General Semantics* (1933, Lakeville, Conn. : International Non-Aristotelian Library Pub. Co.1958 4th edition),

Kripal, Jeffrey J. Roads of Excess, Palaces of Wisdom: Eroticism and Reflexivity in the Study of Mysticism (Chicago: U of Chicago 2001).

Lady L 3rd, *Dancing with Dionysus*, (unpublished mss. BC, 1997) In the possession of the author.

Lady S 3rd, *June 25/05*, (unpublished mss. BC, 2005) In the possession of the author.

Lady Sy 3rd, *September 21 2006*, (unpublished mss. BC, 2006), In the possession of the author.

Lakoff, George and Mark Johnson *Philosophy in the Flesh: The Embodied Mind and its Challenge to Western Thought* (New York: Basic Books, 1999).

Lamond, Frederic, *Fifty Years of Wicca*, (Sutton Mallet, UK: Green Magic, 2004),

Lapatin, Kenneth *Mysteries of the Snake Goddess ; Art, Desire, and the Forging of History* (Boston: Houghton Mifflin, 2002)
.

Leacock Seth and Ruth Leacock, *Spirits of the Deep: A Study of an Afro-Brazilian Cult* (1972, reprinted New York: Anchor/Doubleday, 1975).

Leland, Charles G. *Aradia or The Gospel of the Witches.* 1890; reprint Custer WA: Phoenix Books, 1990.

Levi, Eliphas. *Transcendental Magic : Its Doctrine and Ritual.* trans. and introduction by Arthur Edward Waite, London: Rider and Co, 1896; reprint York Beach Maine: Samuel Weiser Inc., 1970.

Levis-Strauss, Claude *The Savage Mind* trans John
Weightman, trans Doreen Weightman (Chicago:
University of Chicago Press, 1968)
_____*The Raw and the Cooked: Mythologiques, Volume 1*
trans. John Weightman and Doreen Weightman (
1969, Chicago: University Of Chicago Press, 1983)

Lord M 3rd, *27th of June 2005*, (unpublished mss. BC, 2005) In
the possession of the author.

Luhrmann T.M. *Persuasions of the Witch's Craft: Ritual
Magic in Contemporary
England.* Cambridge MA: Harvard University Press 1989.

MacGillivray, Joseph Alexander *Minotaur; Sir Arthur Evans
and the Archaeology of the Minoan Myth* (NY:
Farrar, Straus and Giroux, 2000)

Magliocco, Sabina. Witching Culture: Folklore and Neo-
Paganism in America (Philadelphia: University of
Pennsylvania Press, 2004)

Maphis 3rd and others *Pagans for Peace Tradition Book of
Shadows* (unpublished mss 1991-2008) in author's
possession.

Marx, Karl "Theses on Feuerbach" from *The Marx-Engels
Reader* ed Robert C. Tucker (2nd edition, NY:
Norton, 1978), 143-4.

Maslow, Abraham H., *Religions, Values, and Peak
Experiences*, (1964, revised edition New York:
Viking Press, 1970).

Mathers, S. Liddell MacGregor trans and editor *The Key of
Solomon the King.* London:
George Redway, 1888; reprint New York: Samuel
Weiser, 1974.

Metzger, Deena, "Re-Vamping the World: On the Return of
the Holy Prostitute," *Heretic's Journal* (Seattle) (Fall
1985), reprinted in *Pagans for Peace* 57 (1992): 6-9.

Michaels, Anne. *Fugitive Pieces* (Toronto: McClelland and Stewart, 1996).

Moore, Thomas *Dark Eros: The Imagination of Sadism* (Putnam CT: Spring, 1990).
_____, *The Soul of Sex* (New York: HarperCollins, 1998),

Morgan, Robin, *Going Too Far: The Personal Chronicle of a Feminist* (New York: Vintage/Random House, 1978);

Murray, Margaret *Witchcult in Western Europe* (Oxford: Oxford U. Press, 1921)

Myers, Brendan. *The Other Side of Virtue* (Winchester UK: O Books, 2008).

Niditch, Susan *Ancient Israelite Religion*, (Oxford: Oxford University Press, 1997).

Nietzsche, Friedrich. *The Birth of Tragedy* trans Clifton P. Fadiman (1872, 1927, New York: Dover Publications, 1995).

Owen, Alex.*The Place of Enchantment: British Occultism and the Culture of the Modern.* Chicago: University of Chicago Press, 2004.

Paris, Ginette *Pagan Meditations: The Worlds of Aphrodite, Artemis and Hestia* trans. Gwendolyn Moore (Dallas TX: Spring Publications, 1986)
_____ *Pagan Grace: Dionysos, Hermes and Goddess Memory in Daily Life* trans Joanna Mott (Woodstock CT: Spring Publications, 1990)

Parsons, John Whiteside *Freedom is a Two-Edged Sword and Other Essays* (Las Vegas: Falcon Press, 1989)

Penczak, Christopher *Gay Witchcraft: Empowering the Tribe* (York Beach ME: Weiser Books, 2003)

Rabinovitch, Shelley Tsivia. *An Ye Harm None, Do What Ye Will: Neo-Pagans and Witches in Canada.*

unpublished MA Thesis, Department of Religion, Carleton University, Ottawa 1992.

Regardie, Israel .*The Golden Dawn.* 1941, reprint 6th edition St. Paul MN: Llewellyn Publications, 1989.
_____, *Ceremonial Magic; A guide to the Mechanisms of Ritual* (Wellingborough UK: Aquarian Press, 1980)

Semple, Neil *The Lord's Dominion – the history of Canadian Methodism* Montreal: McGill-Queen's U. Press, 1996

Slater, Norman ed., *A Book of Pagan Rituals*, (1974, 1975, republished York Beach ME: Samuel Weiser Incorporated, 1978)

Smith, Jonathan Z. *Imagining Religion: from Babylon to Jonestown* (Chicago: University of Chicago Press, 1982).

Smith, Robertson. *Lectures on the Religion of the Semites First series The Fundamental Institutions. (*Burnett Lectures. 1889, 1894 2nd Edition London)

Starhawk *The Spiral Dance: A Rebirth of the Ancient Religion of the Great Goddess* (San Francisco: Harper and Rowe, 1979)
_____*Truth or Dare: Encounters with Power, Authority, and Mystery,* (San Francisco: Harper and Rowe, 1987),

Stark, Rodney *The Rise of Christianity – a sociologist reconsiders history* Princeton NJ: Princeton U. Press, 1996
_____ and Roger Finke *The Churching of America 1776-1990 – winners and losers in our religious economy* New Brunswick NJ: Rutgers U. Press, 1992
_____ and William Sims Bainbridge *The Future of Religion – Secularization, Revival and Cult Formation* Berkley CA: U. of California Press, 1985

Statistics Canada, Ottawa, 1981, 1991, 2001 Censuses of Canada.

Surette, Leon *The Birth of Modernism; Ezra Pound, T.S.Eliot, W.B.Yeats and the Occult* (Kingston: McGill-Queen's University Press, 1993),

Suter, Ann *The Narcissus and the Pomegranate: An Archaeology of the Homeric Hymn to Demeter* (Ann Arbor: University of Michigan Press, 2002).

Taussig, Michael. *Defacement: Public Secrecy and the Labor of the Negative* (Stanford CA: Stanford U. Press, 1999).

Thompson. Robert Farris, *Flash of the Spirit: African and Afro-American Art and Philosophy* (New York: Vintage/Random House, 1983)

Tucker, Robert C. ed *The Marx-Engels Reader* (2nd edition, NY: Norton, 1978).

Turner, Victor *The Ritual Process: Structure and Anti-Structure* (1969, New Brunswick NJ: Transaction Publishers, 2007).

U.D., Frater *Secrets of Western Sex Magic: Magical Energy and Gnostic Trance*,(St. Paul, MN: Llewellyn Publications, 2001)

Verter, Bradford ."Spiritual Capital: Theorizing Religion with Bourdieu Against Bourdieu" *Sociological Theory* 21.2 June 2003, 150-174.

Viswanathan, Gauri. *Outside the Fold: Conversion, Modernity and Belief* Princeton: Princeton University Press, 1998.

Wagar, Samuel "An Explanation and Understanding of Wiccan Ritual: Approaching a Deviant Religious Discourse in the Modern West" *Illumine* Vol. 4 Number 1 (2005)
_____"The Wiccan "Great Rite" - *Hieros Gamos* in the Modern West" *Journal of Religion and Popular Culture* XXI (Summer 2009)

Wasserstrom, Steven M. *Religion After Religion: Gershom Scholem, Mircea Eliade and Henry Corbin at Eranos* (Princeton: Princeton U Press, 1999).

Whitehouse, Harvey. *Modes of Religiosity: A Cognitive Theory of Religious Transmission* (Walnut Creek: AltaMira Press, 2004).

Wilson, Barrie *How Jesus Became Christian* (Toronto: Random House, 2008)

Wolkstein, Diane and Samuel Noah Kramer, *Inanna: Queen of Heaven and Earth*, (New York: Harper and Rowe, 1983)

index

samwagar@shaw.ca

Obscure Pagan Press
5-10282 132nd Street
Surrey, British Columbia
V3T 0C7

April 2012 c.e.